Project Management Hacking

How to Manage Projects More Efficiently and Effectively in Less Time

Project Management Hacking

How to Manage Projects More Efficiently and Effectively in Less Time

By
Douglas Peyton Martin
Edited by Lauren Mix

A PRODUCTIVITY PRESS BOOK

First edition published in 2020
by Routledge/Productivity Press
52 Vanderbilt Avenue, 11th Floor New York, NY 10017
2 Park Square, Milton Park, Abingdon, Oxon OX14 4RN, UK

© 2020 by Douglas Peyton Martin
Routledge/Productivity Press is an imprint of Taylor & Francis Group, an Informa business

No claim to original U.S. Government works

Printed on acid-free paper

International Standard Book Number-13: 978-0-367-34896-0 (Hardback)
International Standard Book Number-13: 978-0-367-34815-1 (Paperback)
International Standard Book Number-13: 978-0-429-32862-6 (eBook)

Visit the Taylor & Francis Web site at
http://www.taylorandfrancis.com

To my ADHD, for making me do things faster before I lose focus

on…has that mole on my arm always been that color?

Contents

Foreword

This is typically where the author tries to guilt someone to praise the ingenuity of the book, restate the introduction, and endorse the work with their seal of approval. This takes a significant time and an embarrassing amount of begging to pull off this feat while only delivering marginal value to the finished work. Skipping the Foreword is a prime example of the Hacker path in action.

Preface: Why Buy This Book

THEN

For my generation, hacking was not an evil term associated with identity theft or cybercrime. Hacking meant exploiting a technology beyond the original product's design, finding a novel use for ordinary items, or accessing something without paying. The latter is not a nice (or ethical) thing to do, but this mentality fueled the reduction or removal of cost for a number of products.

I am part of a magical generation that grew up with computers in our homes that were absolutely useless straight out of the box. The only way for me and my friends to get something remotely fun out of an original TRS-80, Commodore Vic-20, or Apple IIc, that our parents spent hundreds of dollars on, was to void the warranty. You could either buy a RAM expansion module for your Vic-20 for hundreds of dollars, or for a few dollars and some electrical soldering, you could go to Radio Shack, order a specific RAM chip to piggyback onto the existing RAM chip, and install it yourself on the motherboard.

Magazines like *ROM, RUN,* and *Compute* published BASIC source code for games and other programs. Rather than transcribing the code and saving it to a cassette, we just changed the portions that suited us. If I wanted to start with 100 lives instead of 3, I just changed that part of the code. If I wanted the game to be easier to beat, I just corrected the flaw in the original design. If I wanted a black background and green characters, I'd change it. My generation was doing this in our adolescence, so we could enjoy our computers, and it has warped how we view the world for the rest of our lives.

NOW

Nearly 40 years have passed since I first learned how awesome it feels to sidestep the hurdles everyone else must clear. I haven't looked back, and I won't apologize for finding the easier path. My favorite principle from *The Agile Manifesto* is "Simplicity – the art of maximizing the amount of work not done – is essential." This concept helped energize my Agile embrace.

Now, I feel it is time to share my knowledge of how to change the rules with others.

A CAVEAT

In no way do I advocate violating any laws or ethical guidelines, like the *PMI® Code of Ethics and Professional Conduct*. This book aims to make the reader a better project manager, helping to focus energy and attention toward the activities and tasks that deliver the most value.

A SECOND CAVEAT

I try not to curse liberally when I write, but to provide honest examples, some terse language may be employed to effectively get a point across. I aim to occasionally shock and entertain to cause you to pause and ponder what is being written.

I am asking you to change your outlook on your career as a project manager, and I will use every trick and tool at my disposal to get my point across. No "F-bombs," but I may say something like "You're getting handed a stick with shit on both ends, so there is no way to handle it without getting dirty" to make a point about a no-win situation with the least amount of effort on my part. I PM Hack my life, including my writing.

ONE LAST CAVEAT

This book expresses my views and opinions. The information contained within is provided without any expressed, statutory, or implied warranties. I, the author, disclaim any liability for any damages caused or alleged to have been caused either directly or indirectly by this book. Throughout this book, I will also be referring to terms such as PMP® or PMI-ACP®, which are registered trademarks of the Project Management Institute, Inc. (PMI) and its *Project Management Body of Knowledge (PMBOK® Guide)* – Sixth Edition.

THE DIFFERENT PATHS: STANDARD, EVIL, AND HACKER

This book attempts to outline the different project management paths we can follow:

- That which our industry standards advocate (Standard path)
- That which the worst of our profession follow (Evil path)
- That which pragmatic PMs follow to maximize the amount of work *not done* without sacrificing quality along the way (Hacker path)

In the spirit of the book's message, the least possible effort will be given to discussing the Standard and Evil paths. Thousands of sources are out there to tell you, the reader, what the *PMBOK® Guide* or the *Scrum Guide*™ are trying to say, so we're going to trust this is not the first book you've read about managing projects, which will save everyone the time of reviewing what should already be known.

We all learned the Standard path, even if we don't follow it. We all know the Evil path, whether we want to admit that or not. It's around us all the time. We may not all be aware of the other path: the Hacker path. Because of this, we will focus our time on the Hacker path, saving us all time and causing no harm. *That* is the very essence of the PM Hacker path!

I just committed to delivering the same value without writing two-thirds of the book, and you just saved two-thirds of the time it would have taken to read the book if it included lengthy discussions of the Standard and Evil paths. A return on investment before the first chapter. You're welcome.

MAJOR SECTIONS OF THE BOOK

- *Getting Certified*
- *Professional Development and Continuing Education*
- *Leading the Project Team*
- *Initiating and Planning Projects*
- *Executing, Monitoring, and Controlling Projects*
- *Closing Projects*
- *General Life Skills*
- *Performs Other Duties as Assigned*
- *Summary*

THE LENGTH OF THE BOOK

I've found that the most informative, entertaining, and valuable business books are short. There is no shortage of 300-page business books sitting in the dollar bin with a picture of some goober with a shit-eating grin on the cover.

This book will not take you through a drawn-out journey that rehashes the same point over and over to look impressive on a bookstore shelf. It's long enough to cover the big points and save you time as a project manager, and part of that commitment is honoring your investment in reading the book and delivering value in the smallest package possible.

With that said, should this book knock it out of the park and be picked up by a big publisher who asks me to "fluff it up" so the spine looks impressive on the shelves, then the second edition won't have this section, and I will dance for the man and write 200 pages if the contract calls for 200 pages, making the first edition a collector's item. Tell your friends. Buy ten copies just in case so you can talk about how great the book was before I sold out and became a hypocrite.

Author

Doug Martin, PMP, PMI-ACP, CSM, CSP, M.P.M., is a senior associate at GR8PM, Inc. and a senior project manager for the Carilion Clinic. At Carilion, Doug has lead enterprise-level projects for over 10 years that span technical, administrative, and clinical systems implementations. Doug works as a freelance writer and Agile coach in his spare time.

Doug is a board member of the PMI Southwest Virginia Chapter. He is certified by PMI as a Project Management Professional (PMP®) and an Agile Certified Practitioner (PMI-ACP®). He also holds Certified Scrum Master (CSM) and Certified Scrum Professional (CSP) designations from the Scrum Alliance. Doug graduated from the American Graduate University with a Master's Degree in Project Management.

Social Media Information:

Amazon Author Central http://amazon.com/author/dougmartin
Linkedin Profile https://www.linkedin.com/in/douglaspmartin/
Project Management Hacking Group on LinkedIn https://www.linkedin.com/groups/8774966/

Introduction

THE STANDARD PATH

There is absolutely nothing wrong with following conventional wisdom on how to lead project teams. Someone has to be the average team member of a PMO or an acceptable candidate in job interviews. Lots of people travel to an exotic island only to eat at KFC for fear of a bad meal or a night on the crapper from iffy chicken at a local establishment. Play it safe and guarantee yourself a spot in the middle if you fear being in the back of the pack. If project leadership is not a calling or long-term career path for you, I would advise staying on the Standard path until your preferred career path opens up.

THE EVIL PATH

I have connections with project managers across the country. The Evil path is not acknowledged in many circles, but none of the following statements or examples of behavior we all see in the profession should come as a surprise. This path is the wrong way to address the project manager's dilemma of too much work and too little time. It violates business ethics, exploits the better nature of others, and fails to win allies for support when the Evil path eventually backfires.

These examples are as generalized as possible, and none are from a single situation. The Evil path is not a great secret, and, unfortunately, it is more common than we'd all like to acknowledge.

Sometimes, project managers deal with challenges in unhealthy ways. It doesn't make them evil as people, but it does cast the profession in poor light. Without solid guidance on how to deal with the challenges we all face, we cannot really fault people that choose the Evil path.

News Alert: I have gone down the Evil path and it absolutely came back to damage me. Calling out these scenarios to show the wrong way is as important as talking about the right way so that we all learn what not to do when stressors put pressure on delivering more than you can reasonably achieve.

THE HACKER PATH

I have worked with a lot of peers preparing to pass their PMP®, and every time I've had the same conversation:

Peer: *"Doug, I've been working on my prep materials, and there are a bunch of things in the PMBOK® Guide we aren't consistently doing that sound like things we should be doing. But, how are we going to do all of them **and** keep working the number of projects we have?"*

Me: *"First, you need to think about the PMBOK® Guide as a toolbox, outlining how to cover the different scenarios that COULD arise on a project so you are prepared to address them. It covers everything you'd need to know to successfully manage a massive undertaking, like hosting the World Cup. We are not hosting the World Cup; we are working at a smaller scale, which means we can safely ignore some of the things that would derail such an event."*

Peer: *"That makes sense."*

Me: *"Second, if we did all the things within the PMBOK® Guide on our last major project, do you think it would have changed the outcome?"*

Peer: *"I doubt it."*

Me: *"Exactly. You need to **know** all of this to work as a project manager and earn your PMP®. You also need to know which processes will impact the outcome of your project. There simply are not enough hours in the day to do EVERYTHING in the PMBOK® Guide to the best of your ability on one project, and odds are you won't have the luxury of working on one project at a time throughout your career."*

If you hold a project management certification, you've likely been on one or both sides of this conversation. It is a shared experience, yet there is little information available to us, in the form of guidance, on how to make these distinctions. Perhaps this quote from a fictional character will provide some guidance:

> "Never half-ass two things, whole-ass one thing."
> —*Ron Swanson from the TV show* Parks and Recreation

For a project manager, the message here is to stop putting partial effort across a bunch of activities. Slim down your focus and do your best with those things that bring the most value toward the success of your projects. Stop worrying about the things that are not likely to influence the outcome of the project.

Keep in mind this approach is a calculated risk, but one worth taking for your sanity and career success. I live by the philosophy that strategically failing at tasks leads to career success. Every day I walk into my office overtasked with no hope of completing every requested activity. I have a few options to consider:

1. *Gut it up and stay as long as it takes to get everything done to the best of my ability.*
2. *Do a half-hearted job at everything so I can leave at a reasonable hour, knowing something is going to bite me in the ass at some point down the road because I didn't focus on half of the things I was assigned.*
3. *Do a GREAT job at the things that matter the most and fail to complete everything else.*

Option one is not sustainable and a quick path to an "it's complicated" relationship status on your social media profile. Numerous studies show the detrimental impact of working extended hours long-term, each revealing that quality suffers first and, eventually, productivity is less than working an honest eight hours. An appealing aspect of XP as a project delivery model is that the team votes to work overtime, which they can only do once a year.

Option two is the option most project managers choose, unfortunately. If your name is on it, you own it and are accountable, regardless of how little effort you put into the task. Accountability is an unforgiving bastard that is going to forget what a fantastic job you did pulling that other project out of the toilet while also managing so many others. It's like a critical mother-in-law, who overlooks all the home repairs you've completed to point out that you cracked a beer before noon.

Option three is the PM Hacker path. Kick ass at the work you get done and leave confident, knowing the work not done is either unimportant or something someone else on the project team can handle.

"I'm sorry I didn't fill out the TPS report, but I was busy getting a key stakeholder to sign off on the change order that will save us thousands of dollars" is a difficult statement for your boss to disagree with. Deliver the projects and the tasks that drive success, and don't sweat the rest. I've yet to meet a project management rock star that attributes their success to a solid PMO process map and task checklist.

A caveat: The Hacker path will fail you at some point. So will options one and two. Some unforeseen risk or issue will lurk in a blind spot created with this approach.

The Hacker path is not foolproof. It is, however, defendable and based on rational thought. Reflect upon failures in your retrospectives and identify if it is a situation likely to happen again. If so, you should spend more energy in that area than you have before. If it's unlikely to ever happen again, then simply apologize, accept responsibility for the issue, and move forward.

Now, let's start hacking!

1

Getting Certified

Credentials like PMP® and certifications such as CSM (there is a difference between the two) bring genuine financial benefit to the credential holder and demonstrate attained knowledge on a subject matter. A large industry has spawned around certification training. Most players are legitimate, helpful, and good value. A few put up a thin veneer of legitimacy with a slick web presence and a similar sounding certification to swindle people with good intentions out of millions every year.

PMP®

The Standard Path

1. Go to the PMI website and read the current credential guide. Satisfy the experience and education requirements with a reputable education provider.
2. Study like a neurotic maniac for months.
3. Sit the exam.

Clean, clear, repeatable; just as the industry standard advocates.

The Evil Path

There are plenty of shady players out there in the PMP® prep world. Beware the companies that know damn well the exam has changed to the new version of the *PMBOK® Guide*, but they still actively market and sell materials for the previous version. A pox on the lot of them for the frustrations and re-test fees unsuspecting newbs have to pay just so they can clear out their inventory before selling the right version of the materials.

Others in the market will report that they have test simulators using "actual PMP® exam questions" reported by "recent test takers." First, I doubt anyone can actually memorize questions during an event as anxiety-filled as sitting for the PMP®, so I call shenanigans on the premise. Second, this is a no-no for anyone who bothered to read the PMI's ethical guidelines.

The Hacker Path

There is no shortcut through the application path. I will share that if you have a toxic relationship with the project "sponsor" or your immediate manager at that time, any knowledgeable stakeholder on a project can serve as the contact on your application. Don't skip a project because you worked with an arrogant jackass, hellbent on making your life miserable, and wait to earn those hours back. Somebody on that project knows you both worked for an all-star asshole and will speak on the organization's behalf to verify your participation.

If you have not learned the valuable life skill of how to take a multiple-choice test, do that first. Most exam questions are phrased in a way that you can quickly eliminate two of the four answers and give you a 50/50 shot. This is a valuable skill that will help you hack your way through a lot of subjects with less than perfect effort. Odds are you, or someone you know, has an SAT/GMAT/GRE prep book, and it is almost always covered in those guides. Crack it open and review the advice it gives on passing a multiple-choice test.

Keep in mind the PMP® is a pass/fail exercise. Time invested beyond the effort needed to safely pass the exam with an acceptable score is wasted time you could have spent binge watching something on Netflix or playing with your children. The PROMETRIC results will only indicate if you passed or failed and provide some generic feedback on how you performed in each knowledge area. No PMP® I know has *ever* looked back at that report once they learned that they passed the exam. Your goal is to get a C+, and the amount of knowledge and preparation it takes to get that is daunting enough.

Some quick things to keep in mind when studying for your tests:

1. *Regardless of how trivial or silly the issue sounds in the scenario given in the exam question, the project manager is always proactive and will act sooner rather than later.*
2. *The project manager will never break the law or act in an unethical manner. The project manager will honor and respect local customs.*
3. *If an available answer is "call a meeting to discuss the issue," odds are it is the right answer.*
4. *Some questions provide the answer to others in the exam. This frequently comes up in the inputs/outputs/tools/techniques questions.*

More detailed tips to help with your exam:

If your PMP® instructor introduced Earned Value Management (EVM) as a subject being "something you just have to learn for the exam. I've never used it and I don't know of many that do," then you likely won't really learn EVM and should ask for part of your fees back. Earned Value Management works IF you commit to the process. Take the time to find someone in your local PMI Chapter, on YouTube, or on another online media platform who is passionate about EVM and has experience implementing it. You'd be amazed at how easy it is to learn when someone with experience using it is teaching you.

As a side-rant: In what other professional endeavor is it acceptable to teach something you have never successfully achieved or believed in yourself? Shame on every PMP® prep instructor who has polluted the opinion of their students from embracing and learning a proven technique that accurately predicts schedule and cost performance because they didn't bother to try to learn and use it themselves.

If we can agree that knowing 80% of the Process Grid's inputs, outputs, and tools and techniques is an acceptable level of understanding for the exam, I have some fantastic news: there is no reason to memorize the entire grid!

The first wave is to identify patterns that are true at least 80% of the time and commit those to memory. Some examples:

- *Initiating and Planning Activities will almost always include Organizational Process Assets and Enterprise Environmental Factors as Inputs.*

- *Monitoring and Controlling – Work performance data is almost always an input. Change requests are almost always an output (with the exception of "Perform Integrated Change Control").*

The second wave is allowing the question to give you the answer and relying upon your ability to read and reason versus memorizing these aspects of the grid. Some examples:

- *The output for the planning activity is the plan for that process. For example, the "Plan Schedule Management" activity will have an output of a schedule management plan.*
- *The input for the monitoring and controlling activity is the activity's plan. Outputs will be updates to the plan, forecasts, and logs of the same activity type.*

The third wave is dealing with the exceptions to the rules and focusing on areas with several activities focused on a specific knowledge area, such as risk. Grids are fine to work from when it comes to presenting visually. However, it is far easier to pass the exam if you actually understand how the activities flow across time, so you can rely upon comprehension versus memorization to know the difference between plan risk management, identify risk, perform a qualitative risk analysis, perform a quantitative risk analysis, plan risk responses, and control risk. If you understand the flow between activities, then the inputs, outputs, and tools and techniques are easy to spot and answer correctly in the exam.

The final wave is to come up with a basic list of activities, inputs, outputs, and tools and techniques to study that simply escape reason (and your ability to remember), and try to memorize. This will be a far shorter list with far less to commit to memory, saving you time studying. It is worth noting that plenty of people who failed their PMP® have a perfect grid committed to memory.

Leverage your PMI membership. PMI members have access to projectmanagement.com. That website has an activity called "PM challenge" with a test bank of 1,000 questions to work through. Any questions missed return to the pool and will repeat until answered correctly. What is genuinely helpful about this service is, right or wrong, the site will explain why the correct answer is the correct answer. Unlike practice exams that need a firm timebox to work in, this can be fitted into a few minutes of slack time throughout the day.

Learn the rules of the proctor organization and how the test instrument functions. In the United States, PROMETRIC publishes an overview of how the test tool will function during the exam. Take the time to familiarize yourself with the tool before sitting for the exam so you're comfortable with the technology.

Also, take time to read the rules to be observed during the exam so you are not rattled when asked to pull up your pant legs and hand over eyeglasses for inspection. When I took my PMI-ACP®, I saw a young woman practically have a meltdown when she had to put her necklace with a locket, containing some of her father's remains, in a locker. I don't know what test she was there to take, but I'd wager she didn't pass and will be paying to re-test.

PMI-ACP®

The Standard Path

1. Read the 12 sourcebooks.
2. Begin using Agile principles in project work to gain experience hours.
3. Take a prep course.
4. Study.
5. Pass the exam.

The Evil Path

In addition to the same shady players in the PMP® prep world, there are an amazing number of Agile "certifications" available. Not all of these are equal, and few have significant value on a resume. There is no way to sidestep a valuable certification by substituting it with a lesser quality title. If it seems too good to be true, it likely is. The Evil path is to go out there and collect "certifications" that fail this simple test:

1. *Can you search for the certification name on a job board and view postings that seek that certification by name?*

The Hacker Path

If you hold a PMP® certification, did you start counting experience toward the certification requirements when you led projects or when your templates were part of organizational process assets? Virtually all PMP®s, actively working as project managers in industries with high complexity and/or high uncertainty, have prior experience working with Agile principles like rolling wave planning, progressive elaboration, frequent retrospectives, or a daily stand-up during some phase of the project.

Use the same pragmatic and ethically grounded approach to demonstrate experience for the PMP® when looking at experience for the PMI-ACP®. Just like the PMP®, make sure you label the activities and aspects of your projects that embraced Agile with the appropriate terms for those activities.

The PMI-ACP® exam will allow an applicant to apply multiple, different education paths toward the education requirement. For instance, CSM credential holders can apply their Scrum Alliance hours toward the PMI-ACP® requirements. Because the PMI-ACP® exam covers a few frameworks, knowing only Scrum is a recipe for disaster. Education hours will likely be satisfied before learning all the frameworks separately.

GR8PM, specifically John Stenbeck, published the *Agile Almanac* series of books. Book 1 of that series is a fantastic PMI-ACP® prep book, as well as a practice guide for successfully implementing Agile on an individual project. GR8PM also offers PMI-ACP® prep courses that cover a variety of blended learning options to split contact between classroom and online learning. Yes, I am part of GR8PM, and yes, I am blatantly plugging the benefits the organization brings to the PMI-ACP® certification path. They're that good.

Preparing for the exam is not as daunting an exercise as sitting for the PMP®. It is worthwhile to reinforce a few key points from the previous section:

1. *Be comfortable with multiple-choice tests.*
2. *Know the PROMETRIC rules and test administration process.*
3. *Focus on simply passing the exam, not on the grade.*

Some additional quick tips:

1. *Focus your time around Scrum, the PMI® "Micro-dynamic Framework," XP, and Kanban. Other frameworks will be touched on in the exam, but not enough to warrant learning them all.*
2. *The Planning Game is an XP ceremony at the start of an iteration. Planning Poker is an estimation technique used to rapidly estimate the complexity of activities. There will be MULTIPLE QUESTIONS on the PMI-ACP® exam that include **both** Planning Game and Planning Poker as possible answers.*
3. *The PMP® exam scenarios nearly always work from the perspective of the project manager. The PMI-ACP® exam scenarios can be asked from the perspective of the project manager/Scrum master, product owner, or development team member.*
4. *Don't skip The Agile Manifesto or the 12 principles in your preparation.*
5. *If the question states a scenario where the team is struggling to work within a constraint of a framework, the answer will be to refer to and use Lean principles to tailor the framework.*

Confusing overlaps in terminology between the frameworks covered in the exam is one frustration with the PMI-ACP® exam. The good news is the test bank questions follow a standard phrasing that either share the role and ask for the appropriate framework or provide the framework and ask for the role.

The big tripwire here is Scrum versus the "micro-dynamic framework," the sanitized framework that looks incredibly similar to Scrum. The two key terms to watch for are sprint (Scrum) and iteration (micro-dynamic); and Scrum master (Scrum) and project manager (micro-dynamic). Clarifying the framework being discussed in the question and the role first is the best strategy.

CSM, A-CSM, CSP-SM, AND OTHER SCRUM ALLIANCE CERTIFICATIONS

The Standard Path

The Scrum Alliance has a solid grasp around the throat of anyone seeking certification through their organization, so the Standard path tends to be *the* path. The organization focuses on face-to-face interactions between trainer and student to maintain standards of quality on the content and validate the value certified trainers bring to the brand.

The Scrum Alliance certifications focus on the Scrum framework. If there is a criticism that could be directed at the Scrum Alliance, it would be that there is little discussion around process tailoring or when Scrum may not be the best solution for the project work.

The Evil Path

It is possible that some questionable Certified Scrum Trainer exists that coaches class attendees through the exams to make sure they pass, but this is not remotely the reported reputation or experience of any CSM students I know. It's also not advisable to take advantage of this type of scenario, should you stumble into it. You'll come up short in the long run if you don't actually know the stuff you're certified in.

The Hacker Path

After the CSM, further certifications require showing work experience in the Scrum framework. Because of the one-note tune from the training material, many Agile practitioners convince themselves that, until their projects are "pure Scrum," they cannot count those projects toward experience. This couldn't be further from the truth. The Scrum Alliance would like to see progression toward "pure Scrum," but they do acknowledge this is a journey for many organizations. If you can outline growth toward "pure Scrum," projects using some Scrum framework principles apply toward experience requirements.

2

Professional Development and Continuing Education

THE STANDARD PATH

For certification/credential owners, professional development and continuing education are mandated. The Standard path is to attend education sessions that count toward continuing education requirements, submit the forms for credit, and pay renewal fees.

THE EVIL PATH

For PMP® holders, there are plenty of opportunities to do things "just for the Professional Development Unit" (PDU). You can launch a taped webinar from projectmanagement.com, leave it running in the background, and have the website submit the PDUs. You can attend a local chapter meeting, sit in the back of the room and play Candy Crush instead of pay attention, and still earn the PDU. In other words, you can scheme the system to log continuing education units, spending little to no money in the process, and keep your credentials current.

This is an asshole move though. Don't be this person. This dilutes the value of the credential owned and brings doubt on everyone with it. It often takes more effort to not learn anything than to participate in activities that will advance knowledge and make you a better professional. Speaking for the presenters at the front of the room at your chapter meeting, we have enough anxiety trying to convince ourselves that our fly is zipped, and everyone is staring at our face and not our underpants without you sitting in the back streaming Porky's. It's an added distraction we don't need.

THE HACKER PATH

Continuing Education Is for Professional Improvement, Not Credential Renewal

Understand that a PDU/SEU/CEU is not the goal of continuing education. Continuing education is to make you a better professional. Challenge yourself and find activities that are outside of your comfort zone to address knowledge gaps. For example, the PMP® assumes that before sitting for the exam you have a base of knowledge in business acumen. If you don't understand corporate finance, meeting facilitation, servant leadership, contract negotiation, risk management, quality management, or other areas most people assume you know, then start there. A solid base of knowledge will make you invaluable to any organization you join.

Seek Activities That Count toward All Credentials/ Certifications Held

This sounds like a no-brainer but, depending on the unique combination of credentials and certifications one holds, this can be tough. Find activities that touch on as many credentials or certifications as possible, and make sure to report them to all credentialing organizations. In other words, double-dip.

Use Activities to Network

If you go to a regional conference or professional development day with coworkers, don't sit at a table with them pissing and moaning about what's happening at the office. Park yourself in the middle of strangers, introduce yourself, and make connections.

When interviewing prospective project manager candidates, the first things I want to know are, in no particular order of importance:

- *Are they insane? (And not "normal PM insane.")*
  - *Are they "black out the eyes in pictures and pin them to a cork board in their basement while listening to overly optimistic pop music" insane?*

- *Are we bringing a high maintenance pain in the ass into the PMO?*
  - o *Will they use meetings to discuss the harmful effects of vaccines rather than projects?*
  - o *Will they attribute my bad mood one morning to my "toxic maple bacon donut's side-effects"? Because that donut, and some miraculous manmade chemicals from the pharmaceutical industry, will keep me out of jail that day.*
  - o *Will they constantly be pushing their lifestyle on me, spewing facts about their gym regiment while concocting their "nourishment" from an assortment of equipment and powders stored in the small laboratory they've assembled on their desk?*
- *Can they find their ass without a map and one hand tied behind their back as a head start?*
  - o *Will I find them walking in circles when asked to step an inch outside their comfort zone?*
- *Are they a good teammate?*
  - o *Will they help the team or be useless?*

The best way to prove your value and that you aren't a headcase is by joining your local PMI Chapter. You'll earn PDUs, build a network, and get to know the folks that will help you get your next job.

Volunteering away from the local chapter is another great networking opportunity. It is especially effective at opening the doors to changing industries, should that become an interest. If you want to move from software development to construction, you might not find a "stranger" willing to roll the dice on you successfully making that shift. But you'll be hard pressed to get turned away from a local non-profit needing help managing their major construction project(s). Go, volunteer, exceed everyone's expectations, and prove you can do it. Build that experience... and network!

Start or Participate in Communities of Practice

Virtually every credentialing organization will count time spent attending or preparing presentations for an internal community of practice if it's related to the certification. Done well, a community of practice will improve the skills for those in its realm. It is also an excellent opportunity to identify and engage internal resources interested in increasing their knowledge and value, preparing a bench of worthwhile candidates ready to step in and backfill an opening.

Plan for One PDU/SEU/CEU a Week

Shit happens. People lose jobs, relatives get sick, you get assigned a project to rescue that has an appointment in your calendar to kick your ass every day for a few months until you bring the project back in order. If you do something silly, like waiting until the last moment to nail down those few remaining PDU/SEU/CEU credits, you will end up in a stressful situation, needing to do something stupid and expensive to stay current.

Commit to an hour a week of continuing education for yourself and your professional development. This commitment will pay you back many times over in discovered efficiencies, gained skills, a growing network, and career advancement.

3

Leading the Project Team

THE STANDARD PATH

There is an abundance of quality works out there on how to lead a project team. *Drive* by Daniel H. Pink is a fantastic contribution to the world on how to successfully lead a project team. Likewise, there is also a fair bit of garbage on the subject that makes a weak case on a flawed point backed by junk science, weak correlations, and incredible bullshit. Be wary of any work that de-emphasizes the value of team members or weaves a tale of snake oil and panther piss on how someone you've never heard of working for a company you never knew existed turned the organization around by smiling more, making the soda machines free, and starting a dream board.

THE EVIL PATH

There are plenty of evil project managers out there manipulating project team members, destroying morale, and doing absolutely nothing to help the team succeed. They cover their ass in insanely detailed documentation for every issue that comes along that points the finger at everyone who is *not* the project manager. Their drive to be successful is at the expense of the teams they lead. They seek personal glory and career advancement, building a Teflon suit of armor to protect only themselves.

THE HACKER PATH

Be a Shield to the Team

A key responsibility for a project manager is to shield team members. Behind closed doors, with the project team, we can talk about anything if we establish an environment of safety and accountability. The concept that transparency should also apply to individuals' issues within project teams and the plans to correct them is a flaw in some perceptions of Agile Leaders. If a retrospective topic touches on an individual and how that individual is going to improve, then that topic needs to stay within the team and not be published to stakeholders. Safety for the project team trumps transparency.

Professional sports team coaches are an excellent example of successfully shielding a project team. When the team loses, great coaches will stand on the podium and say something like, "We lost because I failed to prepare the team to be successful. I will look back at what happened and make sure I adjust my coaching strategy." Behind the scenes, we all know some of the players are going to get a new body cavity courtesy of that same coach who just took all the blame. Every player on that team, though, knows the coach will shield them from external "stakeholders" every time. When that team wins, that same coach, who was the main cause for their loss last week, is suddenly the most minor aspect in the effort it took to win this week, saying, "We won today because of the team and their excellent preparation and attention to details."

Developing and maintaining a reputation as a project manager who will shield the team in times of adversity and stand aside to showcase the contributions of the team members when successful will bring you a currency more valuable than gold: allegiance. People will want to work on your projects. People will know that they will be held accountable in private but protected in public. There is a lot to be said about breeding this type of loyalty.

Establish Norms and Hold the Team Accountable

Accountability sounds like punishment to a lot of people. It isn't. Accountability can be as simple as having someone acknowledge they did not meet the expectations of the team and commit to doing better in the future to meet those expectations. No paperwork, no drama, no calls with Human Resources or the team member's functional manager. It is a simple, one-on-one conversation.

PM: *"Hey Team Member One, I've noticed you've been showing up late for meetings and seem distracted during our discussions. We often must repeat questions to get your feedback. I'm worried the team is going to miss something important because you aren't present even when you're present. What's going on? How can I help?"*

Team Member One: *"Sorry PM, I've been hit with this thing and it's eating up my time with work. I don't know what to do."*

PM: *"What if we addressed your updates and topics of interest first in the meeting agendas? If you get here at the start of the meeting, I'll get you in and out as fast as possible. This only works if I have your focus while you're there, but if we do it this way you can have more time to work on your other project."*

Team Member One: *"Sounds good. Let's try that. Thanks!"*

Nobody is getting papers to sign or marks on their record. Accountability is not about documenting reasons to separate someone from the organization. Accountability is about coaching team members on the actions standing in the way of success.

Some of the norms my teams typically adopt are not incredibly complicated or controversial:

1. *Civil* **discourse is encouraged.** Asking questions or disagreeing with an opinion is *not* disrespectful. Showing someone the respect of talking through differences face-to-face should be rewarded and appreciated by all parties. How else will we learn anything new?

2. **Meetings start on time.** If the project manager is not on time, another team member should be prepared to assume the role of meeting facilitator. NOTE: If you enforce this norm, tardiness for YOUR meetings will be a rare occurrence even if your organization's norms permit rampant tardiness.

3. **Issues are communicated to the *entire* project team as soon as they are discovered.** DO NOT wait until the next status meeting to share an issue.

Norms need to be policed and enforced by the project team, not the project manager. If I am late for a meeting, I love to hear the ration of shit I get from the team and that they started without me. It tells me they're doing their jobs and hold me to the same standard as everyone else.

Your Reaction to Adversity Influences Everyone Else

If you jump around the room like you are walking on hot coals when someone brings up an issue, it raises the anxiety of everyone around you. No project goes perfectly to plan. Every task will not be discovered in planning. Every task will not be completed on time. Unforeseen risks will surface. There is a time and place when shitting your pants is the right reaction, but it can't be your reaction every time something doesn't go as you hoped.

MBWA – Do It

Management By Walking Around is a bit of a passé concept taken literally. Working with virtual teams and remote workers makes this impossible. MBWA is really about making one-on-one connections with project team members away from scheduled team meetings so there are multiple paths of communication to share feedback. Some team members are not confident enough to speak out in a team setting but will share important thoughts one-on-one. If you skip these connections, you miss out on this valuable feedback.

It is also important to have a personal relationship with your project team members. I don't do well with names and thus struggle with the names of the spouses, children, or pets of everyone I work with on a project. There are days I sit in front of an email screen trying to remember the name of someone I have worked with for 6 years. With that said, I do know *something* personal about most of them and use that to maintain a personal connection that lives outside of the project. They like to camp. They volunteer with scouts. They like craft beer. When you visit your team members one-on-one, show genuine interest in them as a person first, team member second.

MBWA is the project manager's best chance to learn of an issue or impediment as soon as it is identified by a team member. Yesterday is the least expensive day to know about an issue, but today will do in a pinch.

The sooner you know there is a turd in the punch bowl, the better your options are for dealing with it.

Encourage Growth within Your Team

Projects nearly always offer opportunities for team members to step outside of their comfort zone and learn new skills. If something difficult or exciting comes up in the project plan, use it as an opportunity to encourage team members to step up and participate in the task. Support them and let them know they are supported, that the expectation is they try to succeed. If they fail in their first attempt, work to get them more support so they learn from the mistake and gain competence and confidence in their abilities.

Are there people on your team with an interest in becoming a project manager? Give them a chance to lead a meeting while you are there. Get them confident enough to lead a meeting when you are out of the office. This helps you both. Invest the time to mentor them one-on-one and put them on the same path someone put you on at some point in your past.

Create Systems and Frameworks versus a Dictatorship

Systems and frameworks do not require the project manager to make every decision. I am typically the least knowledgeable and least valuable member of the project team in terms of understanding the technologies and stakeholder needs we are trying to address. If the project is set up where I am the decision maker on what to do if we have a challenge, we are doomed. For me, systems and frameworks mean setting up the decision-making process driving the project at the team level.

When I worked as an IT Manager, my goal was to prepare and train my teams in a way that they would not feel any difference in operation, whether I was in the office or on vacation. Project teams should have the same lack of impact on productivity and effectiveness if the project manager is absent for a window of time. The frameworks and systems used to manage the project inform the team on how to react and respond to challenges.

Done well, this accelerates the decision-making process, making teams more effective by removing any doubt of objectives or direction needed from a project manager. For the project manager, all the time spent trying to control the project single-handedly is saved.

Agile frameworks genuinely embrace this concept that the wisdom of the team trumps the knowledge of any one leader. In my eyes, this is the crux of what servant leadership is. If you make the smartest person on the project team the project manager (many of you started your career down this path precisely because of this mindset), the project manager is still not smarter than the entire team, collectively. Stop being the hub of the wheel. If you are the hub, you are spinning in circles, getting sick, and lacking the vision of what the wheel is doing and where it is going.

Don't Go All-In on Agile as a Framework or Treat Those Doing Agile Differently

First, we should come to a working definition of "Agile." At best, Agile is vague in our collective understanding. The *Agile Manifesto* and principles are simple enough to understand. When we begin throwing frameworks, processes, certifications, and touchy-feely discussions into the mix, things get complicated.

The primary Agile failure I see within organizations is implementing an Agile framework, like Scrum, on a portion of the organization's active projects, creating a chasm between Agile and traditional, regarding how employees are treated. The principles of servant leadership, Lean, and self-directed teams should be equally applied to everyone working within an organization using Agile anywhere. Agile will fail if we don't honor and respect the wisdom of teams, but the person cleaning the crapper, taking customer service calls, or working on a waterfall project deserves this same consideration.

It's great if we suddenly launch ourselves out of a nineteenth-century perspective on leadership and start trusting and facilitating decision-making, but don't call that the organization's "Agile transformation." That is only joining the revolutionary thoughts on how to effectively lead teams pioneered in the 1940s and 1950s.

When I refer to Agile, I am talking about the product/project management techniques that mitigate the risks of high complexity and/or high uncertainty, by delivering working fractions of the full project scope for inspection and approval to identify and contain the cost of failing to meet customer expectations.

Not every endeavor fits the use case for Agile, and shoving those efforts into an Agile framework creates unnecessary overhead and issues. How the project is managed should be a decision for the project manager, the sponsor, and the PMO, as a whole. Few organizations can defend managing all projects in their active portfolio using an Agile framework.

If you truly want to *alienate and drive discontent within a team*, try to manage a project using an Agile framework with:

- A fully developed implementation plan from a third-party vendor that has been reliably repeated dozens of times and requires rigid adherence.
- Vendor prioritized and estimated "backlog."
- Known and well-estimated work assignments.
- Little opportunity to identify improvement opportunities or free the team to self-direct their approach.

Managing a project like this with an Agile framework only teases a group into believing they have control over aspects of the project that they do not. Be honest about what level of control the team has over the approach of completing the project, and select a methodology that best fits that model. And treat people like you should treat people.

System D

I spent the early part of my career working in restaurants where things rarely go according to plan. I'd wager that things are still as dark, disturbing, and completely amazing as they used to be in the depths of the kitchen. In a restaurant, System D is done to "get the manure back in the horse" and turn a bad situation around so it looks like it never happened, using ingenuity, creativity, and effort.

Some System D examples from the restaurant industry:

- *The prep team shit the bed and did not make any marinara sauce. The recipe requires the sauce to simmer for hours, so we can either wipe out a third of the menu for the evening or come up with a solution. A La Minute (on the fly), we throw some base red sauce in a sauté pan with some smashed up peeled tomatoes, some red wine, and softened veggies and fast cook a marinara to order. It's not perfect, but it will pass.*

- *The kitchen is falling behind, and some godless monster of a customer has ordered the longest make-time item on the menu, a well-done strip steak. A starting baptism in the deep fryer will cut down cook time on that steak and not drag the kitchen deep into the weeds. Think this is gross? I have gotten more compliments on the deep fried "grilled" steak than I ever had when cooked the "right way."*

A System D example from the IT industry:

- *In the development phase of a project, the server suffers a catastrophic hardware failure. Parts are delayed a week because of a typhoon in Southeast Asia and waiting for it to arrive will put the project behind. So instead, "borrow" another server nobody will miss for a few weeks and keep rolling. When the parts do arrive for the project's server, repair it, and the borrowed server is replaced.*

System D on a project is fine as long as we do not impact the quality of the end product. Skipping out on events, like testing, to stay on track is incredibly stupid and usually backfires. A good test for System D being the right compromise is if we would consider it an action where we would ask for forgiveness instead of permission. If we are not afraid that someone will eventually find out what we did to stay on track, then it is a System D solution that should be safe to try. If we know the project manager will be wiping their ass in two places for the rest of their life if somebody finds out what we did to stay on track, we probably need to think of a better solution.

Add FUN to Your Daily Task List

Every minute of the day can't be full of laughter and joy. Projects can be extremely stressful endeavors. In healthcare information technology, some of my projects are literal life-or-death propositions, where the stakes are high and the costs of failure can include lives.

These environments, however, are precisely where some element of play is needed. For example, when I managed field service resources, if we met certain criteria for success that we were struggling to achieve, we set aside Friday afternoons for playing first-person shooter tournaments on our computers. That meant, if our ticket board was clear of high priority repair requests and we did not have requests open for multiple days, we spent an hour or two shooting at each other (which we enjoyed).

This cultivated teamwork to stay on top of those quality goals throughout the week. Initially, we did not pass the mark to play often, but those rare events reinforced the benefit of achieving the goals. Before I ceased leading that team, we were playing nearly every Friday.

There is something cathartic about decapitating an avatar of the boss and bathing in the arterial spray of their blood. Yes, I gave up an hour or two of productivity from each person each week we met our goals, but the return on investment was high. We reduced issue resolution wait times for our clients. We improved communication and teamwork skills. Concrete metrics show the approach worked.

Fun doesn't have to be a violent video game. It just needs to be an outlet for stress that brings the team together to bask in the sunlight of their success. To be a positive driver, fun should be engaging and valued by the project team. For a project using the Scrum framework, if the preceding review meeting resulted in no rejected user stories and the sprint goals are all achieved, why not conduct the sprint retrospective at an establishment that sells adult beverages?

Simplify Documentation

Pre-internet/email, the cost of materials (paper and pens) and time needed to write significantly lessened the volume of communications we were asked to absorb on a daily basis. As a result, any communications sent or received likely contained value and were, therefore, more likely to actually be read and retained.

When email first arrived on the scene and communication volumes exploded, if the subject line or first few paragraphs failed to grab the attention of the intended audience, the whole communication failed because the recipient did not receive the intended message.

Now, people digest communications from a smartphone like popcorn. Attention spans have shortened, and retention is suffering as a result of email and all the other available technology today. Your opportunity to win the attention of your intended audience is now in the subject line and first words of your message. If you're lucky, you get a sentence or two to grab them.

What this means for meeting agendas and notes is the project manager has the limited window of the subject and two or three lines of text to win the attention of the audience. What does this mean for modern meeting notes and agendas?

- **Never send the agenda as an attachment.** There is zero hope it will be opened by everyone, and people will show up to your meeting unprepared and uninformed.
- **Use the "Low Priority" status to stand out.** Almost nobody sends an email at low priority despite virtually all email being low priority. Low priority messages stand out and look unique in everyone's inbox, drawing attention to your communications regardless of what system your company uses.
- **The last meeting's minutes become the next meeting's agenda.**
  o Closed items are deleted from notes to the next agenda.
  o Items that remain in progress have their last status removed from the notes and remain active until it is closed.
  o New items from the last meeting become a new action item on the next agenda.
  o Risks live in the meeting agenda/notes. Only the project manager monitors the risk register. Everyone should be reviewing the meeting agendas and notes, so active risks on the meeting agendas/notes keep them at the forefront of everyone's attention.

Some other everyday hacks for email:

- **Email should be only used after attempts to speak face-to-face or by telephone have failed.** The world has developed a fetish with email, but the time invested in crafting messages and responding to false assumptions is a significant time waster. Speak directly whenever you can. Email only when you must or when you need to send a broad message and no other venues lend themselves to that message in the near future.
- **Name anyone with action items in the subject header.** If a specific person needs to act on the message, put the person's name in the subject of the message to establish ownership in the first layer of processing the message's intent.
- **Avoid multiple requests in a single message.** I have yet to get a satisfactory reply to each question when I have asked three or more

questions in a single message. It simply doesn't work. Send a message for each feedback request.

- *Shutdown a thread after four replies.* Multiple waves of communication become a distraction and are unlikely to be resolved without a face-to-face discussion.
- *"Delay delivery" can be your friend.* Contrary to the thoughts of many, strategically delaying delivery on some messages is better than immediately sharing the message, in some instances. Some examples:
  o An employee is getting shit-canned at 3pm today. Don't wait until after that discussion, when emotions may be charged, to share the news with impacted stakeholders. Take the time to craft the announcement and set the message to send while you are in a conference room telling the employee their fate. In our era of workplace violence, this is a vital step to keep everyone safe and well-informed when this sort of event takes place.
  o You are negotiating with a vendor and need to introduce a time delay in the exchange of feedback to apply pressure. Determine the message and send it later so it is not dependent on your attention at the time you want to share it.
  o Project Activation Updates. If a project is going live and there has been a commitment to regular updates at a stated cadence, then write the update in advance and time the message to send at exactly that time. This avoids a good many calls from nervous stakeholders if the update is late or forgotten.
  o For some stakeholders, being the first message greeting them at the start of the day has the best chance of getting the desired response than any other time. Set these communications with these specific stakeholders to send when they are most likely to respond, even if that introduces a delay from right now.

4

Initiating and Planning Projects

THE STANDARD PATH

A point of clarification: There is a common misconception, even amongst certified PMP® professionals, that the PMI Process Groups I've broken the next few chapters into are the same as project phases. They are not. The process activities are within initiating, planning, executing, monitoring and controlling, and closing overlap. If you are not controlling costs from the first to last day of the project, then you are failing at a fundamental level. If you do think these are phases and not processes, you probably bought my book because you are struggling. The bad news is, I think you have some other things to work on before this helps. Stop reading now and fix this issue, and we'll pick up at this point in a few months.

The chapters are broken down across the process groups because it would be too confusing to do it any other way, but understand that it is not meant to map out things a project manager should only do at a certain point within the project's lifespan.

Depending on the health and maturity of your organization's PMO (or lack of a PMO) and their ability to break out planning activities between portfolio, program, and project management, the starting point of when a project manager is engaged is going to vary greatly. Depending on your abilities to rescue a project from the crapper, you may not always have the luxury of initiating, or even planning, a project.

The book that changed my life on how to set a project up for success is *The Lazy Project Manager* by Peter Taylor. If there is a Standard path to explore outside of PMI's literature, this is it.

THE EVIL PATH

There are a lot of issues that simply cannot be recovered if they are not avoided in initiating and planning a project. Lazy ass-hats that "embrace Agile" because they don't feel like planning give the entire Agile movement a bad name, and their failures poison the well we all drink from.

Likewise, project managers that overtly and overwhelmingly pad estimates because they are unwilling to invest the time in initiating and planning the project correctly create more problems than they solve. Sure, they have safe margins to work within for their special little project, and someone may even pat them on the back and tell them what a great job they did on it, but organizations are not easy to fool repeatedly. Eventually, that project manager is going to lose the confidence and trust of those around them. If you know project managers that jump from job-to-job every 12–24 months throughout their career, then they, at least, are wise enough to realize the charade can't be held up for long.

THE HACKER PATH

Read the PMBOK® GUIDE and Use OPA and EEF

Good, old-fashioned organizational process assets and enterprise environmental factors are the best tools at your disposal. Unless it is the organization's first year in operation, there is a catalog of closed projects and budget performance data waiting for you to leverage. Invest a bit of time reviewing those lessons learned from similar endeavors.

> If the project reuses vendors, you can compare the estimated versus actual costs from previous projects to know if you should adjust their estimates (it will also provide you with the ammunition to make that case).
>
> If the project reuses resources, you can analyze their ability to identify the tasks needed to complete the endeavor, and how long it took them to do it.
>
> If working with a familiar project sponsor, then their projects' artifacts will show their time, budget, and cost flexibility.

Do your homework and use that other *PMBOK® Guide* tool and technique of expert judgment to adjust the feedback you receive versus taking things at face value.

Enterprise environmental factors are a polite way to refer to understanding the unique and fascinating ways your organization is dysfunctional and crippled by incompetence, bureaucracy, and industry requirements. I have an acquaintance who works for a company that uses the "Charlie Brown" rule, which is a polite way to say that if Charlie Brown is on television that month (October through December), the company's board of directors will not meet, and there is no hope of getting a project funded. My friend must hustle to get project approvals from the board by the September meeting or wait until January.

These organizational quirks exist everywhere, so there is no shame in accepting the truth and learning to work around it. The Hacker path here is to observe what happens at the points of dysfunction; note the roadblocks and bumps in the road, when they disappear and for whom. What did that project do to get through a steamy pile of crap without a single stain? Who was involved in resolving that issue? Invest the time to solve these mysteries, use the same techniques on your projects, and know you can wear light-colored pants to work safely every day.

The Project Sponsor Is Your #1 Team Member

Initiating and planning are the starting points of a relationship with an executive project sponsor. This is THE relationship to focus on. I work in an IT department, but I work for my project sponsors regardless of where they report in the organization. For the love of all that is good in the world, do not neglect establishing a strong relationship with the project sponsor. That sponsor is typically a few steps higher in the organizational structure than you. They have a network and relationships you do not. Confide your challenges to them. Ask them for help to get things done. A good executive project sponsor can shave months off a project timeline spending five minutes talking to an old friend and asking for a favor.

Fight for the Right Project Team Members

Nobody gets a team full of rock stars on a project. When the project manager works to acquire resources for the project team, the focus should be given to evaluate the main known factors driving project success. The limited currency a project manager has to influence, cajole, and intimidate resource managers to assign resources should be spent first on the greatest risk and second on the key tasks that drive project success. This sounds like the inverse but think about it: EVERYONE on the project team – every stakeholder, every leader – is going to watch those key tasks and work to make a weaker resource succeed without the project manager spending energy to make that happen. An ad hoc resource, that happens to be working in the riskiest portion of the project endeavor, will not feel the same love and attention. Pack a lunch and sit in the resource manager's office, and do not leave until the risks involved are understood and you are assigned someone who can best attack those risks and make them disappear.

Sometimes, we need to ask for a different player. You may have an asshat on your hands, dragging the team down. You may have discovered the complexity of the work has changed, and you need a more experienced resource to stay on track. Before going to the leader controlling that resource, be an adult and offer them the opportunity to rise to the challenge. Focus on the actions, not the person, and how they are impacting the project goals, then ask them to help you turn this around. If they do not course correct, then escalate and get a new resource. This is vital. It establishes with all stakeholders that you are not going around them the first time adversity strikes, and before you go down the path of consequences, people will get the feedback they need to see that the "pain train" is coming if they do not fix something.

Set the Tone Early

I am amazed when I work with project managers who act like they were just attacked by a swarm of bees whenever there is an issue and also lament the team doesn't keep them updated on how the project is going. The project manager has the greatest influence on the tone and openness exhibited by the project team throughout the project. If there is a risk to public safety or someone spending time in jail then, by all means, lose your religion … at the issue. The person who reports the issue has endured more than enough torture in their own minds before they opened their mouths. Support the person, fight the issue.

Do Not Skip Initiating and Planning for Agile Projects

I know this will anger some people, but on an Agile project I have rarely shown up the day after someone asked me to lead an Agile endeavor with:

- *Named resources with no active engagements or responsibilities.*
- *An approved budget.*
- *A prepared and empowered product owner.*
- *A prioritized and elaborated product backlog to work in the first sprint.*

Some Agilists use the term "sprint zero," but that suggests you have a single sprint to pull something together. Sure, use Agile processes and activities, but don't feel the obligation or yield to the pressure to have a product increment ready to deliver at the end of each early sprint. Proper facilitation of these early sprints sets the team up for success and gets them tooled to have better velocity. These early sprints give your resources time to tidy up other commitments ramping down while allowing you to establish relationships with the product owners, getting them set up for success as they develop the backlog and work with the team to define requirements in terms they will understand.

Planning Does Not Equal a Complete WBS

Hopefully, if you are using Agile, you understand you don't need to detail out every release, epic, user story, and task before starting work on the project. Agile embraces deferred commitment and changing requirements. Time invested planning in great detail, on work that will take place on the distant horizon, is wasteful and silly.

For waterfall projects following a traditional WBS structure, there is greater confusion. PMP® prep materials tend to show a fully developed WBS, and practice activities attempt to fully develop a WBS, when, in reality, the day the WBS is completed is the day the project manager closes the project, not when the first task starts. Again, planning is a process, not a phase. This trips up executives, PMO Directors, and project managers all the time. Plan what you can accurately predict and reliably anticipate. As soon as you move from a SWAG (Scientific Wild Ass Guess) to a WAG (Wild Ass Guess), it's time to stop and accept you don't know enough to make a meaningful estimate of that element of the project.

At regular intervals, review the areas that are not completely identified at the first attempt to plan the endeavor, and continue to progressively elaborate and develop it.

Budget to a Not-to-Exceed Level

Budgeting is not a time to bargain hunt or negotiate aggressively with vendors. The timing of when the project is approved for funding and kicks off is typically unknown. Market forces can swing between budgeting and approval. A bargain today may be impossible tomorrow. Budget at a price that goods and services are attainable any day of the year.

The Project's Contingency Is for Unforeseen Risks

If there is a known risk to the project's success before the budget is finalized, then for piss-sakes, dig your head out of your ass and account for it in the project budget. If the project has no available funds when an unforeseen risk comes up because you blew it on some gold plating nonsense that now threatens the success of the project, options are limited to:

1. *Eating a shit sandwich and asking for more funds to complete the project.*
2. *Spending human capital to overcome funding shortages.*
3. *Eating a grilled shit sandwich and negotiating reduced scope or extending timelines with the sponsor.*
4. *Doing something catastrophically stupid like cutting quality or cutting costs recklessly elsewhere to make up for the additional expense.*
5. *Calling a meeting at sunrise, face the sponsor and project team, and admit to your disgrace, slice your abdomen open so your intestines fall out, and have your deputy project manager behead you.*

Go After the Biggest, Highest Priority Projects in the Organization

This sounds counterintuitive. Aren't we supposed to be talking about getting out of the office early and working less? Why would any sane person go after the biggest projects with the most visibility in the organization? Because it is the biggest project with the most visibility.

If you manage the most critical projects in the portfolio, you get a ration of shit in terms of stakeholder management, attempts at scope creep, and panicked team members crapping their pants at every issue. However, you also typically get the pick of the litter for team members, guaranteed focus from stakeholders and leaders, and instant assistance with resolving identified challenges and issues. Excellent team members with plenty of experience make any project endeavor simpler, and that is typically what is assigned to a project that simply cannot fail. Top projects have the focus and attention of leaders and stakeholders. Everyone reads your status reports. People will call you, offering to help with issues and risks outlined in the status reports.

People magically show up to your project meetings when the project is high profile. You will rarely hear a bullshit excuse like "I couldn't work on the project because I had a carbuncle in the crack of my ass lanced and had to lie on my stomach for a week." In other words, the GAAB factor is lessened, and sometimes that is the thing requiring the most time. For those unaware, the hidden process group missing from PMI documentation is GAAB – Grown Ass Adult Babysitting.

Planning to Close the Project Is the Number One Planning Activity

If you work in an organization with a project closure checklist, you should have a copy of it open and active for every project you manage. If you do not, then you should be thinking about how to close the project from the first day it's assigned. Focus on project closure and solidify acceptance criteria into objective measures from the start. This brings knowledge transfer and operational ownership of the project post-activation to the front of everyone's minds.

When digesting feedback or challenges, the number one question in the project manager's mind should be "What happens after the project closes?," and it should not disappear until the answer is clear and well communicated to all stakeholders. If a challenge or issue is isolated to the project, the project manager should spearhead the resolution. If the challenge or issue extends beyond the timespan of the project, then someone else likely needs to be identified to take ownership of resolving the issue.

Start Your Retrospectives Now

One crucial failure of traditional project management thinking is waiting until the project's end to conduct a retrospective and capture lessons learned. If a project is a temporary endeavor to deliver a unique product or service, then why, in the name of all that is good in this world, does convention say to wait until the end to figure out how to do that better the next time? If it is truly unique, there is no next time.

For the next project, lessons learned can only capture improvement opportunities at the thematic level. For this project, lessons learned can make everything left in the project plan better. Whether the project is Agile, hybrid, waterfall, or written out on stone tablets, set up regular retrospectives now.

Sometimes You Need a Sponsor AND a Champion

The sponsor of a project is often an executive requestor seeking a change from the current state. A project champion is the respected, evangelical force selling the organization's stakeholders on the need to change the current state and is highly engaged in the project's activities to provide guidance and set the tone for the endeavor. Sometimes the sponsor can also be the champion, but it frequently can be a recipe for disaster. Someone has to be the voice of change stakeholders will respect and respond to their call to action.

If the sponsor is too busy to be engaged in the regular activities of the project, you need a champion. If you are not sure who the champion is on your project, it is the poor bastard staring at you in the mirror every morning. The project manager should never be the champion unless the project happens to be for the primary benefit of the Project Management Office.

Nobody gives a squirt of fly piss about a communication from me in my organization outside of my project team members or, possibly, my own department. Without a champion, the project manager is assured to work long hours and will have low engagement and high resistance to change when it comes time to deliver the project into the hands of stakeholders.

5

Executing, Monitoring, and Controlling Projects

THE STANDARD PATH

This is when the work "gets done." Most in the industry advocate spending the most time and focus in this area of project management. There are more books, podcasts, webinars, and articles on this dimension of project management above all others. This is where most project managers spend the majority of their time, focusing their care and attention.

THE EVIL PATH

The Evil path involves doing some stupid things in the name of finishing the project on time. Keeping a project on track is basically the entire point of your job as a project manager, but there are galactically moronic measures for which there will be no understanding or forgiveness.

The Evil path involves steps like signing change orders with the vendor to crash resources without having the funds available in the project budget, timing those orders so the invoices drop after the project's activation. Or it involves cutting short or eliminating testing or inspection events that are technically optional. Those escaped defects will be found by customers. Asshole project managers will do this then stand in a command center at go-live and admonish team members for not finding that issue before the activation.

―――――――――――

THE HACKER PATH

When the #$!* Are We Saving Time?!

I haven't really given back much time at this point in the book, and that was the promise on the jacket. So, is this another empty-themed business book that sits on the shelf, read once, invoking a case of buyer's remorse every time it is seen, moved, and eventually donated to charity or outright put in a garbage bin? I hope not.

THIS is when the project manager saves time. If we have set the project up for success, then it is time to lay off the throttle and let the stars on your project team shine. It is time to transition to coach and stop playing a position on the field of play. This section of the book is where time-saving is found, but it only works if all that work and effort is put in to set the project up for success from the start.

Do Nothing That Gains Knowledge of the Product

I love technology. I love to learn new skills and solve difficult problems. It is also a giant pond of quicksand between me and the exit to my office. Project managers disconnect at the end of the project and move on to the next endeavor. If the project manager is working toward completing tasks that improve the product or increase knowledge and understanding of how to support the project, then the project manager is screwing the rest of the project team. In other words, you can't lead AND work on the project. This is that "don't half-ass two things, whole-ass one thing" concept.

Are you getting calls about projects that closed a few years ago because you are the only one that knows how to fix something? Are you resolving technical issues? If so, you short-changed the opportunities other project team members had to learn the product being delivered, and they are now less prepared to support the system after the activation.

If you have your nose down, working on a specific part of the project, then you are no longer looking at the big picture. Your vision is limited, issues are going to pop up elsewhere, and if you keep playing the project's savior, you are going to dive into another problem and end up putting the project even further behind. It may feed your ego to tell the world you rescued the project with your awesome abilities, but it does little for the project team's conviction, as it implies you lack confidence in their ability.

Your job as a project manager is to identify those challenges, advertise to stakeholders and useful resources for assistance, then move on to the next thing. In other words, the project manager should focus on the transient tasks that provide zero residual value to the product being delivered.

This is a trap virtually every project manager finds themselves in early in their career. Few project managers start their careers purposefully to manage projects. Get the ever-loving hell out of this trap if you are in it. You are not helping the project succeed. You are not able to handle as many projects as you could if you learned to let go.

Do Not Fear Raising Issues

When a project begins work toward delivering the product or service planned, I immediately place the project at risk on any status report or risk report I present. Virtually, all activities to deliver the scope lie ahead of us, so how can I conceivably say the project is "on track" even if the first 5% of the project's planned work is going as planned?

Encourage the reporting of issues and risks as soon as possible and reward that behavior with support and assistance. Those stakeholders, sponsors, and leaders reading your reports and attending your meetings need to understand the project world is messy. Don't hide how the sausage gets made from the people you need to rely upon to deliver resources and assistance to keep things on track.

Do you want to try a new career or change jobs? Outside of committing a criminal act, the fastest way to do that is to show an "all green" status board on a project, and then pull an 11th-hour problem out of your ass that was known to you for a while, but never showed up in a status report or project team meeting's notes. Be transparent, be assertive, and intervene early. The cheapest day to know about an issue was yesterday, but today ain't bad either. Stay in front of the issues and keep everyone that you think cares about the project informed about them, and what you need them to do to turn it around.

The longer issues fester, the bigger they get. The bigger they get, the more time it takes for the project manager to resolve. Be aggressive on impediments and issues. I can hope Justin Bieber never releases another record, but hopes do diddly shit to make something happen.

Cut Your Status Meeting Time in Half

The concept of plenism applies to all meetings. Plenism is a perspective that nature abhors a vacuum. If you schedule a one-hour meeting to cover the right way to scratch your ass, the team will spend an hour debating the up-and-down approach, the side-to-side approach, the spiral approach, and the bear-on-a-tree approach. Odds are the meeting will end with no clear answer, and a committee will be formed to clarify if we are talking about bare-handed scratching or using a tool for the job. Basically, if you ask for an hour, the project team will spend an hour talking about whatever you want to talk about. If you ask for 30 minutes of their time, they will edit their engagement to fit their updates into the allotted time. Don't think you can half your meetings? Sit down and read through the meeting notes out loud and convince me why the meeting needs to be that long using the 5-whys technique.

Most organizations have tracking tools that dramatically reduce the need for extended status meetings. I can look at software and ascertain the status of every project I manage, and my organization is hardly mature with leveraging technology to track project tasks online. The meeting is not to discuss what sits on a tool that the entire team can look at any time. The meeting is to cover what isn't there. What are the issues, impediments, and risks, and how will they be addressed?

Meetings are time removed from the team's productivity and your time to work on other things. They also cost a shit-ton of money to the organization. A one-hour meeting with 20 people takes 20 hours of productivity off the table every week it is held. If benefits and salary are at an average of $50/hour/person, you are eating through a thousand dollars a week to talk about recent vacations and things everyone already knows. If the project runs for a year and we miss two meetings for holidays, then it costs $50,000 to hold that meeting. Save the company a new compact car and make it 30 minutes.

Already at 30 minutes? Try 15 minutes for a couple of weeks. Are you "Agile" and holding a daily scrum for 15 minutes? That's awesome, but keep in mind you're using 75 minutes a week for the stand-up, if the stand-up runs the full duration. The Agile daily scrum is timeboxed to 15 minutes, but that does not mean you MUST spend 15 minutes a day in that meeting. What if we did a ten-minute daily scrum? Would we miss anything?

The gift Agile gives us is everyone attends the daily stand-up, and if there are topics that require more discussion, then only those with a stake in the topic stay to discuss it in a sidebar or arrange a time to discuss it later. This pressure valve gives the ability to set a typical cadence and duration for a meeting with the ability to discuss a topic in more detail, if needed, with just the people that need to engage on that topic.

When should you stop cutting time? When you start feeling as if you and the team are not informed on the status of the project, or there is a need to have a sidebar discussion on a regular basis because the timeframe of the meeting does not allow the bandwidth to cover typical updates. Hold at that length, try to condense the format, and if you must, go back to a longer duration.

The Commitment to Change Is Not a Marriage Proposal

I am amused at the reaction of most people learning Agile concepts for the first time about the team's capacity to learn from failure and change its approach through the regular retrospective. A significant hurdle for some people is the concept that the team might change its approach at the end of each sprint.

Within the Scrum framework, the team's commitment to a change in process is the next sprint. If they determine things are better in the next review, they may solidify their commitment longer or talk through process improvements.

On any project, we should be evaluating how to improve our process, but resistance to change frequently holds us back from improving what we are doing, even though everyone recognizes the shortcomings.

Encourage your project teams, sponsors, peers, and leaders to embrace change and the willingness to experiment and try a new approach for a week or two. If it is iffy, ask someone, doing a segment of the work not on the critical path for the next week or two, to try out the change and share how it worked out during the next retrospective. At the end of the experiment, check in and see if things are better or worse. If things are better, secure everyone's willingness to go forward doing things a new and better way. If things are ambivalent or worse, go back and applaud everyone for being willing to change.

Ignore the Noise, Listen for the Silence

I don't leave a brown stain in my underwear over risks or issues generating significant chatter and activity from the project team, sponsor, or other stakeholders. Everyone can see and smell the dumpster fire. The team's focus is on putting out the dumpster fire, so there is no need for the project manager to sit around worrying like somebody licked their lollipop when they weren't looking. It is known, it clearly is understood, and it is being worked. Mission accomplished.

What should concern the project manager is what the team is not talking about; what they are *not* focusing on. What have they assumed is not a big issue that really is? Monitor what is on the team's plate and ask probing questions. If an area of the project is under control, people will give detailed answers that quickly satisfy your curiosity. If an area is a Greek tragedy waiting to be discovered, you will get vague feedback or attempts to redirect.

Focusing on the silence keeps everything on the near horizon in focus. It is genuinely counterintuitive, but vital to avoiding crashing the ship into a giant shit-berg lurking under the surface to sink the project.

Stay Focused on Closing the Project and Conducting Regular Retrospectives

Stay on top of this. Keep that closure form around so you focus on the acceptance criteria outlined, avoiding scope creep, and maintaining knowledge transfer and operational readiness to support that new product or service.

Keep those retrospectives rolling, even if everything comes back with no big outcomes a few times. The project team will remain energized and focused, knowing you're interested in hearing their feedback. The sponsor and stakeholders will know they have an engaged project manager, willing to make changes to keep the project on course.

Know How to Spot a Dry Well

This is a tough subject. Not all projects are meant to succeed. Going through the motions, spending your organization's limited time and resources, and hoping it works out in the end is a poor use of time and money on everyone's part. Killing a project before it is completed is a difficult decision, but it is one of the most valuable contributions a project manager can make to their organization.

Emotions and an attachment to sunk costs cloud decision-making. Let's assume it is 2012, and we have a statement of work to develop an application for Apple IOS, Android, and BlackBerry. Three months into the engagement, we recognize BlackBerry's market share is in a death spiral. Do we continue to sink money into the third product or fold the BlackBerry effort, focusing on accelerating our time to market for Apple IOS and Android? This is a simple answer from the outside looking in. Judgment gets clouded when:

- *Emotions take over because the team working on the BlackBerry development is well-known and full of nice people.*
- *The millions spent by the organization on a BlackBerry development department with staff, equipment, and infrastructure make it difficult to walk away.*

Here, the project manager has an advantage over virtually all other stakeholders in the decision. The project manager can focus on the value the project is going to deliver at closure, asking the right (and tough) questions to ensure the organization is allocating the best resources toward the best outcomes.

Project terminations or failures are not a reflection of the sponsor, the organization, the project manager, or the project team. If you forecast the project is headed to the crapper and do not share it because it is an uncomfortable discussion, you are a shithead. As a project manager, your obligation to all parties is to make unemotional assessments of the project's viability and allow the sponsor and other stakeholders the opportunity to act on that feedback.

A project manager frequently has much in common with the responsibilities and limitations of meteorologists. They monitor recent developments, project future outcomes, and report what will likely happen next. They can't, however, change the weather.

BlackBerry's market share fell off a cliff in a matter of months. Great organizations saw the crash and halted and redirected those efforts toward Apple and Android to improve those products and grow their market share. Those organizations' awesome BlackBerry developers could learn new skills and pivot to a new technology. It is more compassionate to help identify the market shift and change direction early to give folks the opportunity to learn a new skill. Staying the course means the company could fold because they can't recover from further sunk cost and those BlackBerry developers fall further behind having marketable skills, putting their careers in danger.

The Daily Issue/Risk Resolution Meeting Is Undefeated at Solving Issues

Projects in jeopardy due to a serious issue or risk are a common challenge. Organizations often take extreme measures to address the challenge by cutting resources, giving ultimatums, slashing scope, or sacrificing quality.

All these approaches have a dubious record of success and create long-term damage that is not easy to recover from. An approach that does not create long-term damage, however, is scheduling a daily status meeting at a time that is not comfortable for the team to attend. That doesn't mean it should be uncomfortable for the project manager though. As an early riser, my morning go-to time is 7:30 or 7:45am for a daily meeting. It creates no hardship for me, but since it is not an ideal time to have a meeting, it motivates the team to put the project back on course to eliminate this daily time commitment.

The daily issue/risk resolution meeting is different from a daily Scrum on an Agile project or the regular status meeting for a waterfall project. The topic for the daily issue/risk resolution meeting is the specific issues generating risk to project success and what is being done to resolve it. When that challenge is resolved, the risk meetings end, and regular meetings resume.

I wish I could give you some scientific breakdown from the works of Hertzberg or Maslow that proves the logic behind the phenomenon, but I cannot explain why this works so well. It just does.

Silicon Valley firms have proven this effect by offering a number of "perks" to their employees that are really social engineering hacks to trick employees into working longer and harder without feeling negative about it. They do benefit the employee, but they benefit the organization overwhelmingly more.

By providing free or nearly free meals in their onsite cafeteria, with breakfast being offered from 6:00–7:30am and dinner from 5:30–7:00pm, they can lure employees onsite sooner and/or remain later than normal business times and net some additional productivity. To the employee, this sounds awesome, but is it worth a bagel, banana, and some bacon to come to work earlier or stay later? Damn Skippy, it is! Is it worth providing lunch onsite so staff are not leaving and spending twice the time to eat compared to eating at the office? Yep. Is it worth a few dollars for an onsite meal in exchange for those extra hours of productivity? Absolutely.

Setting the time to a less-than-pleasant window at the beginning, middle, or end of the day ensures the team is either starting their day early, staying through lunch, or working later until the challenge is resolved. Disrupting that daily routine will not be well received, but it provides a solid motivation for resolving the challenge so normal routines can be resumed.

The forced meeting also puts peer pressure on everyone working to resolve the issue. Nobody wants to show up to this discussion, say they did jack shit to fix the challenge, and be the reason we have to meet again tomorrow. Everyone present wants this to end, and they know the criteria being applied to consider the issue resolved, so the discussion can stop taking place.

The key formula here is that this is a temporary measure and only used when the project is at serious risk of success. Establish and agree upon the requirements to end the meetings with all participants. Invite and demand participation from the entire project team and leaders those team members report to. Publish daily notes to all stakeholders so everyone is aware of the challenges, what the team is doing to resolve them, and what everyone can do to help.

6

Closing Projects

THE STANDARD PATH

Most of us are so delighted when a project is nearing an end we move through closing as fast as we humanly can. Invoices paid? Check. Sponsor signature? Check. Retrospective? Let's schedule one and run through the agenda as fast as possible.

PMI and other thought leaders focus on the technical aspects of closing out invoices, signing acceptance documents, closure forms, and other artifacts.

THE EVIL PATH

Some project managers will do some incredibly silly things to get a project closed so they can stop losing sleep at night. The worst choice is taking a victory lap at the go-live, playing the douche-card to the sponsor of "That's a change order and it will take thousands of dollars to add that feature" to something that obviously should have been included but wasn't specifically noted in the scope. Another douche-card play hoses the project team with "This thing that clearly should work but was not caught in user acceptance test is now a post-live issue. I'll log a ticket, but it is on the support team to fix this."

I'm not advocating to eat every gripe and groan during, and shortly after, activation as something the project team should absorb, but rejecting everything so the project can be closed as soon as possible is a genuine dick move. It will sour the relationship with your sponsor, and anyone working this project will be annoyed to see your stupid face if they end up on another project with you in the future.

THE HACKER PATH

Focused from the Start, No Biggie

Closing the project is about solidifying relationships, not getting invoices paid and freeing time on your schedule for the next project. If you have been focused on the acceptance criteria to close the project and kept everyone's focus on closing the endeavor, there should be no 11th-hour surprises that add a new phase or cause a debate on what constitutes "productive use" to sign the closure form. Pay yourself back and use this time to solidify relationships and make the next project easier.

Solidify Your Relationship with the Team

The project manager has the big stick and can swing it a few more times to set everyone up for success. I tend to withhold praise. I'm a generation removed from participation trophies and the self-esteem movement. Doing your job shouldn't involve getting a high-five every time you manage to not shit the bed the night before you come to work. If you're like me, closure is when you need to break these rules even if it feels stupid and saccharin.

Thank everyone on the project team and make sure you do it in a fashion that it is known to the team member's leader and their leader in the organization's structure. If there are some opportunities for that person to improve, share it, but do it in a separate discussion and make that one-on-one. This is a good opportunity to also ask your team member for feedback on how well you supported the team, taking their words to heart and thinking about how to improve for next time.

Solidify Your Relationship with the Vendor

For the vendor, make sure everything is paid. If there are ongoing maintenance fees, make sure they know where those bills need to go moving forward. Thank the entire vendor group, including the vendor's leader. If the project went well, offer to co-publish a white paper for their marketing needs, or serve as a reference site for potential customers.

Peer reference calls are a networking activity. Do not miss the boat and blow off a reference call because that project is in the past. A project manager is going to be on the line from that peer organization. You may want to work at that organization one day. Give solid, honest feedback, connect on LinkedIn or some other platform after the call, and maintain that relationship moving forward. Offer to talk again if they have additional questions.

Solidify Your Relationship with the Sponsor

Resist the temptation to be curt with the executive sponsor during closing. Most people remember the end of the journey better than the beginning. The sponsor should love you and hate the project if things go awry. Piss-poor product? Talk about how much worse it would have been if you did not have their support and guidance and the pressure being applied to the vendor to correct the glaring issues.

Happy sponsors are a major addition to your network moving forward. You will need their help with something down the road. How they feel about you will influence whether your request is at the top or bottom of their list or forgotten altogether and never completed.

This relationship must include the sponsor's administrative assistant. I have seen peers twist on that nipple the wrong way, and it is not a fun place to be moving forward. For most organizations, admins rule the corporate structure. If I have an email from my CIO and an email from the CIO's admin, each asking for me to do something, I work the admin's request first. Admins are continuously engaged with their assigned executive. They have the most facetime and influence on the opinions of their executive. They control access to that executive's calendar and many screen and prioritize emails. Crapping on the admin puts you in a position you cannot easily recover from until that admin leaves.

7

General Life Skills

THE STANDARD PATH

There are shelves and shelves of books and thousands of websites dedicated to helping people become successful. I can summarize darn near the entire section with a single statement:

"Get a good night's sleep, manage your time wisely, treat people like people, and leverage the skills and talents of those around you."

THE EVIL PATH

This is pretty simple. The Evil path is when you use people for your personal gain and the equation always adds up in your favor. An easy experiment to see if you are on the Evil path would be to approach ten coworkers and ask them, "Hey, do you have five minutes to drop me off at the garage to get my car sometime this morning?" Score yourself based on how many people agree without reservations.

0–3 – You are evil incarnate. Turn your life around or you will die alone.
4–5 – Meh. You have some positive qualities, but chatter behind your back is probably not supportive.
6–7 – Cool. If you collapse, crap your pants, and pass out, someone will likely still perform CPR on you.
8–9 – You are killing it on the EQ front and have good relationships across the board.
10 – You lying dillweed.

THE HACKER PATH

Work an Offset Schedule

I normally work 6am-ish to 3pm-ish. The rest of my department normally works 8am–5pm. This approach has several advantages:

1. *My commute is 20 minutes shorter a day than working 8am–5pm. That's 100 minutes a week I'm not stressing out in traffic as the rest of the drivers check their Twitter feed instead of watching the road.*
2. *I work with executives and physicians that also typically start their day between 6am and 7am. If I need to get on their calendar, I have an instant path that is typically open each morning.*
3. *I have two hours to focus on tasks requiring uninterrupted time to complete. If I knock those out before project teams start work, I'm available to work with them on impediments and issues without feeling frustrated that they are pulling me away from the things I need to do.*
4. *Nothing motivates a team working through a serious issue like an inconvenient daily call to talk about that issue until it is resolved. A 7:45am daily status call mysteriously makes things happen more than hollering, crying, or encouraging. It has never failed to resolve a challenge I've faced.*

The same benefits can be realized working 10am–7pm, if you are a late riser or if you'd like to visit the gym before work, as long as the majority of the executive stakeholders and project sponsors you interact with are able to work with you within that schedule.

Stop Digital Grazing

Digital grazing is what I refer to as the practice of continually checking work email after work hours or on vacation. I've worked with people that have been as responsive to communications on vacation as they were in the office. That's not a vacation, that's working from an expensive remote office.

If you are forever tethered to work by a rectangular ball and chain in your pocket, then you have nobody else to blame but yourself. Set boundaries but set them both ways. If you are at work, work. If you are away from work, check in with your friends on Facebook; tweet and post on pictures of your dinner to Instagram; talk with your spouse face-to-face over a three-minute discussion about whatever you otherwise would have spent the afternoon texting with each other. These distractions drag down your productivity at work.

Show up to work, focus, kick ass, and go home. When you are at home, kick ass at being the best spouse, parent, friend, coach, gamer, or whatever it is you are doing away from work.

Stop Being a Work Martyr

Short bursts of working 12-hour days to bring a crucial task home may be a necessary evil, but on a normal week, stop working more than 40 hours.

The EU has implemented a 48-hour maximum work week. There is a study[1] from Australia that advocates a three-day work week if you are over 40. An unbelievable amount of studies has been done on this topic over more than 100 years and they all hit a common theme: After 35 to 40 hours, you are wasting your time.[2]

Multi-Tasking Is Bullshit

Think that's wrong? Then time yourself doing two things.

Pass 1 – Write the two lines of text below, one entire line at a time.

```
M U L T I T A S K I N G
I S B U L L S H I T ! !
```

Seems pretty simple, right? What's the big deal? OK, now try Pass 2.

Pass 2 – Write the same two lines, but this time write the first letter on the first line, then the first letter on the second line, then the second letter on the first line, then the second letter on the second line, and keep that pattern until both phrases are done.

```
M U L T I T A S K I N G
I S B U L L S H I T ! !
```

So, how did that second pass go? Did you have any errors? How much longer did it take? Task switching is a waste. If you can't write two words without confusing your brain, you sure as goose shit cannot efficiently focus on multiple, complex knowledge work tasks at the same time.

If you interview anyone that says they are a "multi-tasker," give them this test. If they can do Pass 2 faster than Pass 1, hire them right then and there.

Do not play the ADHD card with me. I peg the meter on the ADHD spectrum. I can take 32 mg of amphetamines at bedtime and sleep like the dead. I may take less of a penalty to task switch thanks to my off-center brain chemistry and desire to run into a burning building, but the penalty is still there. Embrace the Agile principles of WIP limits. Do a personal Kanban board if nobody else will listen to reason, but limit the times in a day you shift focus.

Foster Relationships outside of Your Comfort Zone

Within your organization, a project manager interacts and connects with other leaders more than those just inside their own department. The cornerstone of your internal network is previous project sponsors and executive stakeholders. Cherish and maintain these relationships. My company's COO used to be an HR Consultant that was a key stakeholder on a project. If I call him, I will address him by his first name, and he will respond the same way.

These C-Suite executives, Vice Presidents, and other senior leaders can help you with your career. You have proven you can get things done on their projects. Once these people are established in your network, you should try to give at least two favors for everyone you request in turn, and the request needs to be when things are serious and worthy of their time.

It isn't a card I play often, but these leaders can bail your ass out of a river of shit. They have resources and influence you cannot hope to command, so if the project is at a crossroads between utterly screwed and just knackered with some help, make the call. When the dust settles, show your gratitude and make sure you return the favor two times before you make that call again.

Outside of the organization is where I think most people utterly fail to work on their relationships and their network. Your friends in the local PMI Chapter are likely not hiring managers in their organization. They can put in a good word, but they can't offer you a position.

No position is bulletproof. You should be evaluating the other organizations within commuting distance and fostering relationships with people that work there. Parachutes only help if you are wearing one when you get shoved out of the plane.

So far, this doesn't sound like brain surgery, does it? Stay in touch with your old sponsors and stakeholders. Reach out and make a name for yourself in your city. This is where things start to get fun, but so many people are intimidated they never get past the first two phases.

The final phase is to meet and get to know your heroes. Did you like a speaker at a recent conference? Have you been trained or coached by someone you respect? Have you read a book by a best-selling author that you like? For some unknown reason, would you like to connect with me? Is there a company you'd love to work for? Then sack up and get to know them.

I'm writing this book because I stayed after a PMI Chapter meeting, shook John Stenbeck's hand, and told him I'd love to be an early reviewer for his next book. That turned into a co-authoring gig and a multitude of other opportunities. Smarter people than me ran out the door and didn't take a moment to shake John's hand.

Speakers, authors, coaches, and trainers are well-traveled and well-connected. Secure those relationships. Promote their posts and activities on your social media feeds. Bring your value and your unique talents to their doorstep and ask how you can help them.

Not every attempt will succeed, but I promise you will be surprised at how many will. Once you have made the connection, monitor for opportunities where you can offer them value, and strike when you see the opportunity to shift from a follower to a partner.

Continuously Seek Opportunities to Be More Efficient and Effective

Complacency is a cancer that will eat at your career. If you think you are awesome and have everything figured out with no reason to change how you approach work, then you are categorically insane. The more I learn about the profession of project management, the more I find people with a far better method, and I realize I still don't know most of what there is to learn about this art and skill we all practice.

Your situation is not a snowflake. Plenty of people work in the same industry doing the same job, facing the same ridiculous shit you do every day. Find them. Talk to them. Be willing to teach them some of the things *you* have figured out and listen when they tell you how they handle a situation *they* have figured out.

I feel the annual performance evaluation is a worthless endeavor, but it is how most organizations structure pay increases and advancement, so it is a situation to tolerate and accept. However, that should not be the tool used to chart growth opportunities for you as a professional.

Sit down and work out a four box. List all of the regular things you spend time on within the four boxes.

	What Brings Value	
What Takes Time	High Time Low Value	High Time High Value
	Low Time Low Value	Low Time High Value

Then do some simple analysis.

	What Brings Value	
What Takes Time	Stop doing this dumb shit. Ask for the value. Show the organization that the effort spent to do this dumb shit is soul-draining and make someone agree it needs to stop happening.	Seek ways to do this more efficiently and effectively.
	If it must be done, delegate it or put the least possible effort into the endeavor. Start asking why this must be done and try to eliminate it from your regular routine	This is currency to trade with peers. Publish how you are doing this and share it with peers so they will help you with your challenges.

Continuously Work to Absorb a New Project

The next project can come at any time, so why do so many project managers absolutely fail to prepare for it ahead of time? From the moment you are assigned a new project, your goal should be to adjust your typical daily workload to absorb another new project. That means you should not rest until you are comfortable leaving early on a typical day. Not on time; early.

Do this and the next project is not a death sentence to fun or a healthy work–life balance. When I am in a pattern where I can reliably leave early, I can invest more energy into individual relationships with the people working on my projects. That way we'll have a better connection and better lines of communication to discuss and work project impediments and issues.

Does this feel like cheating? It shouldn't. Project management schedules have plenty of 12–16-hour days out there. It has plenty of days when an executive sponsor needs to meet outside of business hours. Project management has plenty of days when a call needs to be made during lunch because a vendor is in a different time zone.

Being ready for what comes next on a project is a core competency for project managers, yet we rarely apply this to our personal lives. If you are not comfortable enough with leaving 20 minutes early on a random Thursday, how can you possibly be comfortable taking a vacation and not worrying about work while you are gone?

Know When to Give 80%

"I give 100%, all the time" is the dumbest shit anyone can say. What is the fastest you can run 100 meters? Can you run that fast for a 5 K? What about a marathon? Can you really give 100% all the time? If you do, then you are headed for a nervous breakdown.

Here's the fascinating truth if you work as a project manager. Odds are that only a handful of people, outside of your peer project managers, can even tell the difference between you giving 80% and 100%. You have two projects starting at the same time. One is high priority, high visibility, and has a budget of $10 million. The other is low priority for a single business unit with a budget of $30,000. You should not be allowed to use sharp cutlery if you give equal effort working on the charter for both projects.

Continuously Scout, Apply, and Interview for Dream Positions

Projects are tricky endeavors. The right project going the wrong way can end your employment, even if you have done everything possible to make the project successful. Your position is in the danger zone of the organization for restructuring or cost cuts.

If your dream is to retire to Naples, Florida, then use the tools at your disposal like Indeed or LinkedIn to search for your dream job in Naples, starting today. Do not fall into the false belief that landing a dream job is no big deal. Dream PM jobs in your industry, in your preferred location, are not frequent occurrences. Applying at every occurrence dramatically improves your chances of making that move a reality. It can take years, with multiple occurrences of no interviews, being dropped at the screening interview, or going to the final round of interviews but not being offered the job before that move happens. If you covet that position, then plenty of others are likely vying for it as well, both inside and outside of that geographic area. You may not be the #1 candidate the first try through an organization, but if you perform well in the screening process, they will talk to you again and again on future opportunities. Do not block or ignore an opportunity because you missed the cut for an interview or an offer last time.

Publishing Is Interviewing

Contributing to the body of knowledge of your profession is an unsolicited application on the desk of any hiring manager who reads your article, blog, or book, or watches your webinar. Platforms like LinkedIn allow everyone to publish and share your perspective with the world.

You may not be an expert in everything, but I guarantee you are an expert in something. Share it with the world. You will be amazed at the direct messages, network additions, and opportunities you will field.

Punish Yourself for Working Late, Reward Yourself for Leaving Early

I have lost over 70 pounds over the past couple of years. I plan to go to the gym every day. Gym time need not be wasted time. You can listen to podcasts, watch webinars, and really work on continuing education while you exercise to maximize your investment in yourself from both a knowledge and health perspective.

When I leave work late, I still work out. I may simply increase the intensity, so the workout is harder to make up for less time at the gym. If I leave work really late and can't make it to the gym, then I will go home and work with kettlebells for an hour. Kettlebells are not remotely fun or enjoyable, so it is the activity I look forward to the least.

For you, the rules would differ. The idea is to reward yourself for staying focused and getting through the day on or ahead of time and provide yourself some negative reinforcement when you fail to meet that goal.

If you have your schedule under control, apply the reinforcement model to another major goal you are working toward to help keep that primary goal in focus.

Learn to Negotiate

Negotiating contracts with external entities is a business acumen skill that project managers should possess before they earn their PMP® in the eyes of the Project Management Institute. Little energy is put forth to cover these topics for certifications or within their published standards. It is amazing how few project managers genuinely know how to negotiate.

Getting the contract right has the potential to save you more time than all the other points covered in this book. Failing on a crucial contract term is a prime root cause for cost overruns, missed target dates, piss-poor quality products, and the project manager "seeking opportunities outside of the organization." Spend more time than I cover in this book on this topic as a continuing education focus, but here are some key points:

Beware of the Low Bidder

Low bidders rarely finish the job at the price they bid. They frequently have iron-clad language on deliverables and a low threshold of changes that will result in a change order at an additional expense. The low bidder on a recent contract I took over to rescue was a "low bid." Reading through the contract language, it clearly stated the cost was an estimate and the actual cost would be at a time and materials rate. When I took over the project, we were already over $200,000 deep in change orders over the original estimate.

Low bidders are frequently desperate. Desperation can be beneficial if the bidding organization is ascending in size and reputation, and they need to prove they can succeed in an organization like yours. A company in decline is desperate to keep the doors open to their business. Saving a few nickels with a company edging toward bankruptcy is a risk with a decent chance of costing far more if the company folds.

Contracts Are Risk Management Agreements

The purchaser and seller have risks to consider when entering an agreement. Contracts declare which party accepts risks in a given situation.

Contract Type	Purchaser Risk	Seller Risk
Fixed Price	The purchaser may overpay for services rendered if no major issues are encountered during execution. *Purchaser should review scope and change order process.	If more time or resources are needed than planned, the company can lose money to deliver the project. *Seller should clarify the scope and define a clear change order process to understand the acceptance criteria for payment. *Raw materials/supply cost fluctuations risk profitability.
Fixed Fee + Actual Cost of Materials and Labor	Profit to seller is transparent. *Risk of cost variance in raw materials/supplies is assumed by the purchaser. *Risk of additional time/effort to complete endeavor is assumed by purchaser.	*Time over the planned effort reduces the relative profit of the endeavor, but the organization is assured a profit margin for the agreement.
Time and Materials	Most risks are assumed by the purchaser. *A good idea only if the complexity and uncertainty are known and well understood. *Consider phase gate reviews with the option to terminate the agreement to control risks.	The risk of non-payment or early termination are high if cost overruns occur and deliverables are not achieved. *Frequent invoicing and status reviews should take place to isolate the amount of the contract that could go unpaid or contended.
Contract Rider – Cost Incentive/Penalty for Meeting/Missing a Target Date	A good idea if time is a premium constraint. *Quality is at great risk with this sort of agreement.	Not all delays are in control of the seller. Consider language to secure engagement and set feedback deadlines and resource commitments from the purchaser.

Contract Terms Worth Fighting For

1. *State of Enforcement*
   a. Both parties want this to be their home state. If things nosedive into the outhouse, this is the state the contract dispute is likely to be heard if it goes to a court of law.
2. *Arbitration/Non-Disclosure*
   a. Arbitration is fine in principle. In practice, it can genuinely suck the life out of both organizations working through a dispute. Who gets to select the arbitrator? Is their decision final and binding, or can you still go to court? Are we bound to an NDA during arbitration, until the matter is resolved, or forever? Customers have a bully pulpit with peer organizations and can influence other potential customers away from an organization IF they can talk openly about their experiences. Look at Yelp as a platform for griping about poor service in a place of business. What if you had to sign an NDA before you ate somewhere that prevented you from giving a one-star review? Would you still feel eager about trying the blue plate special? How confident are you feeling about a good meal? You should have the same concerns with a vendor demanding silence on a potentially negative outcome.
3. *Travel/Meal Reimbursement*
   a. People who travel for business have little comfort for their trouble. Unchecked, they can rack up impressive costs for airfare, lodging, and meals. Get specific on the classes of expense covered (coach airfare, midsize sedans, $X/night hotels, $Y/day meals) and demand to see actual receipts. I failed to do this on a project years ago and one entitled little douche put the project $20,000 over budget eating surf and turf dinners and sleeping in the executive suite.
4. *Change Order Process Thresholds and Scope Definition*
   a. This is the battleground where projects are won and lost. Both parties should have a vested interest to establish a strong mutual understanding of what each party needs to accomplish to satisfy the terms of the agreement. Both parties have a vested interest in defining the threshold in cost/effort when an unforeseen need is either absorbed and worked in

good faith as part of the endeavor, or when it will result in a change order at an additional cost.

5. *What About Price?!*

   a. Price is a frequent point of contention on agreements, but it should be the LEAST important factor in most agreements for the majority of the negotiation. Here's why: Sales commissions are nearly always based on the price negotiated and not the terms. The sales rep for the vendor will gladly add conditions and adjust terms as long as you are not reaching in their wallet. Leverage that mindset to win all the contract terms and extras you can get. When you are confident there is no more room in terms and conditions, then you can work on price. Price should always be the last point negotiated for this reason.

Verbal Commitments Are as Valuable as Poo-Stained Underwear

Beware of the verbal commitment sales trap that countermands the contract. Virtually all contracts include a clause stating the contract supersedes all other commitments and is the sole binding agreement. Once that contract gets signed, salespeople become remarkably scarce and forgetful about anything discussed verbally. By the way, you should consider emails and text messages as verbal commitments.

Silence Is a Powerful Negotiation Tool

Try this the next time you buy a car. Test drive the one you want, have the salesman value your trade, price the vehicle, and estimate your payment on an offer sheet. Say nothing for five minutes, then gently ask for your desired changes of terms.

The salesman will leave, come back with a revised sheet that is not your request, but better than the original sheet. Say nothing for ten minutes, then ask for your same desired terms again. Repeat with longer windows of silence and the same desired terms until you feel things are the best they will be. Silence is more powerful at times than any other technique.

Sellers hate silence. If they are publicly traded and nearing the end of their financial quarters, they will work miracles to get a signed contract ahead of that date. Responding to offers with silence will often spur a better offer with no additional effort on your part, other than patience.

Being a Great Project Manager versus a Great Spouse/Parent Is a No-Brainer

You can be both a great project manager and a great spouse/parent, so this is not an absolute choice, but there are tradeoffs in our everyday lives. I work for a healthcare organization, and my work frequently places me in the path of patients nearing their life's end. I see plenty of family members wrenching hands, stress eating bad hospital cafeteria food, and losing sleep over the fate of their loved one. Sometimes a person's coworkers are on the same path, but do not confuse coworkers with the company.

I have former coworkers I care more about than family, and whom I would not hesitate to stand by, get in trouble with, or dispose of a body for. That's further than I would go for anyone in my family, other than my wife. I'm not talking about friends you work with; I'm talking about the company you work for.

The company values your contribution, but not you. The company is designed and structured to go on without you at a moment's notice. Your family would be devastated for years without your presence.

Do not make the strategic failure of putting work ahead of family. I do not know what the divorce rate is for project managers, but anecdotally it appears to be pretty high. In the worst of scenarios, it is far easier to find a position that respects a healthy work–life balance than going through a divorce.

Insane, ridiculous nonsense will always try to tug at you to stay longer at work. As you grow and improve in competence, you will work more challenging endeavors with greater prominence and more issues to resolve, so don't fall into the trap of "this will pass with time." Your spouse, partner, children, family, and pets are not guaranteed to always be waiting on you when you get home. At some point, they will give up on expecting your presence and go their own way. Cherish your time with loved ones. Fight for that time above all other endeavors and use the remainder of your available time toward work, not the other way around.

Learn to Facilitate Meetings

Knowing how to facilitate a meeting is another business acumen skill PMI assumes all project managers know how to do, so it is not covered in detail, but a surprising number do not. I highly recommend reading one of the works Ingred Bens has developed on the subject as a continuing education endeavor, but I will make a poor attempt to summarize this topic in a couple of paragraphs.

Determine the Meeting Type and How to Facilitate It

1. *The Announcement – Here is some shit you need to know.*
   a. *Questions to Ask*
      - *Do we really need to have a meeting just for this, or can we cover this in another venue?*
      - *Do we expect to field questions? If so, try to plan for likely questions and prepare an answer.*
   b. *Approach*
      - *Share the news. Get everyone to acknowledge they understand the news by asking a couple of attendees to paraphrase the message.*
2. *Status Updates – How are things faring with the shit I have assigned you to work on?*
   a. *Questions to Ask*
      - *Do we really need to have this meeting?*
      - *How can we shorten this meeting if we need to have it?*
   b. *Approach*
      - *The agenda should have an entry for each person to give their update with a time box for their update, so no single person monopolizes the time available.*
      - *All issues and risks should have a clearly assigned owner.*
3. *Problem Solving – How are we going to get this shit done?*
   a. *Questions to Ask*
      - *Do we really need to have this meeting?*
      - *Should everyone be present, or at least be video-conferenced in, so we can all see the same whiteboard/tools/presentation materials to provide adequate feedback?*
      - *Are we SURE the participants are empowered to make decisions to resolve the challenge? If not, don't waste their time or insult their intelligence by working on a solution nobody will act on.*
   b. *Approach*
      - *Determine how to capture and address:*
        1. *Defining the problem that needs to be resolved.*
        2. *Brainstorming the potential root causes of challenges.*

3. *Prioritizing those potential root causes.*
4. *Brainstorming solutions to the top two to three root causes.*
5. *Prioritizing the available solutions based on the highest impact to resolving the challenge.*
6. *Identifying ownership for each selected solution.*
7. *Inserting these new assignments to the project plan/ product backlog for tracking purposes.*
8. *Inserting the assignments to meeting agendas to monitor progress.*
9. *Assessing if you can objectively facilitate the discussion and remain neutral, or if you need a peer to facilitate so you can participate in the discussion?*

4. *Bad News Announcements – I have a cat turd sandwich. Everyone is going to take a small bite so we all do our fair share to make it disappear.*
   a. *Questions to Ask*
      – *Who should give the bad news?*
      – *Is it really bad news for everyone or just a handful of impacted stakeholders?*
   b. *Approach*
      – *Get everyone present in person and video conference ONLY participants physically unable to attend in person.*
      – *Share the goal of the project.*
      – *Share what has happened that will result in bad news so everyone knows why.*
      – *Share the bad news.*
      – *Solicit questions from participants.*
      – *Ask participants to paraphrase the news and how it impacts their work on the project so everyone understands the message.*
      – *Thank everyone for their continued support.*

END NOTES

1. BBC News: *Three-Day Working Week* "*Optimal for Over-40s*" https://www.bbc.com/news/business-36069754, April 18, 2016
2. LinkedIn: *Rules of Productivity* https://www.slideshare.net/flowtown/rules-of-productivity-2756161 December 21, 2009

8

Performs Other Duties as Assigned

THE STANDARD PATH

It is a reflection of our modern times that most of us work under a job description with a final entry stating, "Performs other duties as assigned." Few organized workplaces can cleanly divide work to round numbers and not generate slack time or resource gaps, so this statement covers the need to ask all of us to step outside of our lane and do something extra from time-to-time.

The Standard path for professionals asked to take on work outside of their normal lane is to accept the task like a Christmas gift of woolen socks from grandma and do what they can to make it go away as soon as possible. People have enough to do, so it is understandable that being asked to take on some additional responsibilities can be frustrating and not necessarily embraced as an opportunity.

THE EVIL PATH

There are some sinister little shitmongers in the world that will manipulate situations so that they never end up taking on additional responsibilities. They have a Filofax (millennial readers, just Google it) full of reasonable, weak-ass excuses that prevent them from doing anything other than their stated position. These people are rarely promoted, rarely satisfied in their roles, and about as interesting as a documentary on the mating habits of flies.

THE HACKER PATH

Learn the "Yes, and..." Technique

If my boss wants me to clean the shitter, I'll clean the shitter. If my boss really wants me to step outside of my normal lane and help the organization, my answer is always going to be "Yes, and...." Anytime I'm asked to do something I am not normally assigned or not entirely comfortable with, I will answer, "Yes, and you understand that means X may not happen." X is the lowest priority or most annoying shit you've got on your plate at the moment. Essentially you trade the thing the organization needs help with the most for the thing you find of least value.

Saying no is just stupid. Your leader has a perspective a step above you, and it is not your job to judge the best person for a job or the value of a request for your time. Trust in their judgment and assume the request is urgent, of value, and needed.

Saying just yes is even dumber. Doormats are stepped on, covered in shit, and thrown out as soon as they show wear. Do not become a doormat and blindly take on new work unless you truly are not fully tasked and feel the desire to take on something new.

"Yes, and..." is a healthy dialogue and negotiation tactic. You are not unwilling to take on a new challenge, but we need to accept some things either aren't going to happen or will be the first thing dropped from our attention if a choice needs to be made between the new task and the current payload.

Organizations that wisely identify and promote leaders from within recognize time is limited, and a key factor in being "ready for what is next" is being capable of recognizing the requests of value and making the right sacrifice for time and attention. As a leader, you have the ability to tackle, delegate, or drop a task. You are being asked to tackle a task. Any leader with an awareness of the role recognizes you will either need to delegate or drop something else in order to complete the new request. If your leader does not understand this dynamic, then you may be in a toxic situation with a dark end in sight.

Keep in mind this is a negotiation and not a declaration. If your consequence doesn't pass a prompt approval, it is time to talk through other options. You may not get to drop a complete project or task. Perhaps we can agree that, as a project manager, I simply will have less time to dedicate to each project. The rule to follow is you should not say no, but the discussion doesn't end until your boss says yes to some concession.

This takes time and practice to master. Applied consistently, your boss will be up-managed and prepared to have that discussion before knocking on your door and they may have some recommendations of their own for what can change.

Volunteer for Additional Work Strategically

Every organization has endeavors that sustain the viability of the company and those that disrupt the status quo and transform the organization. Try to steer your career, and your time, toward the disruptive projects.

Here is the blunt and simple reason why: The opportunities to be negatively judged are higher on a project to keep the train running. If you are remodeling the bathrooms in your office, there are few features you can add that will delight folks in the context of a crapper. There are a multitude of things on that project that will disappoint stakeholders. Air blowers or paper towels? It is a no-win situation. You can convince people to change religions easier than their preference for drying hands. Automatic flushers? They better purge every turd from the bowl every time because touching that button once will be considered a failure compared to touching it every time on a manual flush throne.

New endeavors have little history associated with them. Flaws are understood and expected in ancillary systems and features. Think about this: The space program didn't think to design a means for an astronaut to go to the bathroom in their first design of the Mercury space capsules. The Gemini capsules considered the issue enough to put plastic bags on the spacecraft, but most would not consider that a resolution to a clear opportunity from Mercury.[1]

The focus on disruptive projects is on the aspirations and core goals of the endeavor. The focus on sustaining projects is on the mundane. One can absorb complete failures in ancillary goals. The other can have no blemishes or it will be considered a failure.

Do Not Hose Your Teammates

You cannot dump crap on your teammates as a consequence of stretching outside of your normal scope of engagement. Keep your teammates aware of any additional work you are taking on and ask for their advice on how to approach it regardless of whether you need it or not. Your teammates will give you some words of caution and advice worth listening to, and they will not feel ambushed by another project assignment while you are out there on the ragged edge. It arms the team with important intel on what everyone is working on.

Learn to Spot the Turd Hunt

There is no nice way to put it. Sometimes you get pulled into a turd hunt. A turd hunt is a search for shit that will never matter and never turn into anything other than a turd. The end result is you gather a nice gallery of turds for display, and the requester remarks on the skill exhibited to retrieve the turds and walks away. It is a task with no value and no real actionable outcome other than the work.

You can't leave a turd hunt. It is required you bring those turds back for inspection. You must be supportive and show allegiance to your fellow turd hunters. The questions here for you and your compatriots on the prowl for ass nuggets are, where shall we source the turds, and how much effort shall we put into the turd arrangement for review by the requestor?

The secret to the turd hunt is getting all parties, EXCEPT for the requestor, to agree that it is a turd hunt. The turd hunt team then puts forth the least possible effort to create the façade of a quality turd safari while investing the least level of effort to finish the task.

A common turd hunt is to read a business book then discuss it as a peer group. I fully recognize the irony of this statement, but this book is based on honesty, even if I mock my own work in the process. Virtually every bullshit business book you are forced to read covers every conceivable topic in the preface, the foreword, and the first and last chapters. The rest of a turd hunt book is 200 pages of making the same case dozens of times over. If the last chapter makes you wish you had read the rest of the book, by all means, read it.

This approach to business books is rock solid. There are even services out there that summarize business books, so you don't have to read it.

Odds are, your Vice President is a customer of that service, and the book you are reading for the organization had a good summary from the service and the soulless monster hasn't even read it. Why? You don't sit in the Vice President's office of a corporation without knowing how to navigate a turd hunt.

If the requestor is satisfied, we have been a successful posse for poop. And yes, sometimes the entire project is a turd hunt.

END NOTE

1. Space.com: *The Scoop on Space Poop* https://www.space.com/22597-space-poop-astronaut-toilet-explained.html, August 29, 2013

9

Summary

WHAT'S NEXT?

For the most part, summary chapters are a means to pad the length of the book and to make the same points that, hopefully, should have been easy enough to understand if the author did their job the first time. Here is a bullet point list that should capture the spirit of this book without rehashing specific points.

- *STOP half-assing everything you do to get it all done. Slay the things that move the needle, and stop doing those that drain your will to live.*
- *Get certifications that bring value to your career, and use your continuing education to actually learn some new shit and meet some new people.*
- *Look out for your team, and they will look out for you.*
- *Invest time and energy into good planning, solidifying your relationship with the project sponsor, and setting expectations of performance with the team.*
- *Coast on a project in motion, cut your meeting times in half, and monitor where nobody else is worried about the big bad risk that could derail the project.*
- *Take care of your sponsor when you close the project, and you have a powerful ally to help you on your future projects.*
- *Show up early, leave early, get better at what you do, leave work at work, and meet your heroes.*
- *Trade the thing your boss needs you to do now with the thing you dread doing the most.*
- *Tell your colleagues to do the same. If they don't know where to start, tell them to read this book.*

Index

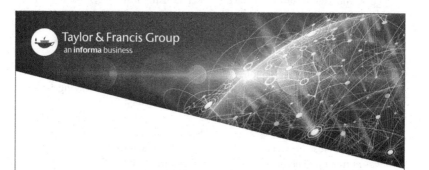

Printed in the United States
by Baker & Taylor Publisher Services